Kingdom Dating 1

Spiritual Dating for Citizens of the Kingdom of God.

```
I0145114
```

"As it is written, I have made thee a father of many nations, before him whom he believed, even God, who quickeneth the dead, and calleth those things which be not as though they were." Romans 4:17

2

Dexter & Petula Jones

UWriteIt Publishing Company
Goldsboro, NC USA
http://www.uwriteitpublishingcompany.weebly.com
http://www.soulmatesolutions.org

Kingdom Dating 1 by Dexter & Petula Jones
Copyright © 2013 Dexter & Petula Jones

ALL RIGHTS RESERVED

ISBN-13: 978-0615793245 (UWriteIt Publishing Company)
ISBN-10: 061579324X

First Printing – April 2013

NO PART OF THIS BOOK MAY BE REPRODUCED IN ANY FORM, BY
PHOTOCOPYING OR BY ANY ELECTRONIC OR MECHANICAL MEANS,
INCLUDING INFORMATION STORAGE OR RETRIEVAL SYSTEMS,
WITHOUT PERMISSION IN WRITING FROM THE COPYRIGHT
OWNER/AUTHOR

This publication is designed to provide information in regard to the subject matter
covered. It is published with the understanding that the authors are not engaged in
rendering legal counsel or other professional services. If legal advice or other
professional advice is required, the services of a professional person should be
sought.

Printed in the U.S.A.

"Now therefore ye are no more strangers and foreigners, but fellow citizens with the saints, and of the household of God." Ephesians 2:19

"But seek ye first the kingdom of God, and his righteousness; and all these things shall be added unto you." Matthew 6:33

"Now faith is the substance of things hoped for, the evidence of things not seen." Hebrews 11:1

"Through faith we understand that the worlds were framed by the word of God, so that things which are seen were not made of things which do appear." *Hebrews 11:3*

"To whom also he showed himself alive after his passion by many infallible proofs, being seen of them forty days, and speaking of the things pertaining to the kingdom of God." Acts 1:3

The Power of the Spiritual Realm

And when Jesus was entered into Capernaum, there came unto him a centurion, beseeching him, And saying, Lord, my servant lieth at home sick of the palsy, grievously tormented. And Jesus saith unto him, I will come and heal him. The centurion answered and said, Lord, I am not worthy that thou shouldest come under my roof: **but speak the word only,** *and my servant shall be healed. For I am a man under authority, having soldiers under me: and I say to this man, Go, and he goeth; and to another, Come, and he cometh; and to my servant, Do this, and he doeth it. When Jesus heard it, he marvelled, and said to them that followed, Verily I say unto you, I have not found* **so great faith,** *no, not in Israel. And Jesus said unto the centurion, Go thy way; and as thou hast believed, so be it done unto thee. And his servant was healed in the selfsame hour. Matthew 8:5-10, 13*

Table of Contents

Introduction

Dedication

We thank God for the grace and mercy he has bestowed upon us in giving us the ability to write books. Not just any books but books that will bring about a change in the lives of people. Also, we dedicate this book to our precious daughter Jasmine, honey even though you're not dating yet, when the time comes here is kingdom dating information so that you will not have to be in the dark about God's method of dating as so many other individuals are.

Also we dedicate this book to our son Brandon, son in all your ways acknowledge God in your dating choices and he will direct your paths.

KINGDOM PRAYER

And it came to pass, that, as he was praying in a certain place, when he ceased, one of his disciples said unto him, Lord, teach us to pray, as John also taught his disciples. After this manner therefore pray ye: Our Father which art in heaven, Hallowed be thy name. **Thy kingdom come,** *Thy will be done in earth, as it is in heaven. Give us this day our daily bread. And forgive us our debts, as we forgive our debtors. And lead us not into temptation, but deliver us from evil: For thine is* **the kingdom,** *and the power, and the glory, for ever. Amen. Matthew 6:9-13*

Introduction

This book is a spiritual book and it will be hard for a carnal believer or a non-believer to understand. This is not your ordinary book about dating and relationships. Because it is a spiritual book the ones that will get the most out of it are believers in Christ Jesus. The word of God says, *"But the natural man receiveth not the things of the Spirit of God: for they are foolishness unto him: neither can he know them, because they are spiritually discerned."* *1 Corinthians 1:14*

As a citizen of the kingdom you are called to live by your faith and operate in the realm of the spirit. A question that I would like to start off asking you is; do you believe that you can meet your Soul Mate within the next 30 days? If there is any hesitation at all in answering that question in your heart then for you it will not happen. However, if you can answer that question with an immediate response without any hesitation in a positive manner then get ready because this is your year. If you were not able to answer that question immediately in the positive then your mind has to be renewed and this is the book that will help transform it.

If you desire to be married and have been single for 5, 10, 20 or more years it is because you have not learned how to tap into the spirit realm and cause your mate to come forth. You have been living more in fear and doubt than in faith and belief and you have reaped the rewards of your fearful thinking.

Either you're living your life in faith and attracting the mate of your soul or you're living your life in fear and experiencing no potentials or are simply just dating with no real potential in sight. Most singles are living in fear and the thoughts which are deposited deep in their spirit are thoughts such as:

- It's hard to find the right person.
- I wonder will I ever get married.
- All the good Christian men/women are taken.
- Blah, Blah, Blah, etc...

When you live in fear it creates a magnetic field that pulls to you the thing that you feared. Job said, *"For the thing which I greatly feared is come upon me and that which I was afraid of is come unto me." Job 3:25*

As a single person that desires to be married you must stop operating in fear, fear is of the devil and it causes uncertainty and a feeling of doubt about what you're asking. You must get rid of the spirit of fear, that spirit that causes you to be afraid, anxiety, panic, trepidation, uncertainty and distrust. The Kings manual (the Bible) says, *"For God (the King) hath not given us the spirit of fear, but of power, love and a sound mind." 2 Timothy 1:7*

As a citizen of the Kingdom it's time to learn how to date in the spirit realm for your mate and live by the faith which never fails. When you date in the spirit realm you call those things that do not exist in the natural realm but does exist in the spirit realm to become a material reality in your life. The word of God says, *"Even God (you must begin to act just like God), who quickeneth the dead, and calleth those things which be not as though they were." Romans 4:17* It is time to cast aside the doubt and fear and begin to live in belief and faith where there is unlimited blessings and liberty in the spirit.

No matter what you may have believed or witness in your life in the past as far as relationship is concerned I want you to know that you don't have to live the present reality you're living; you can create a new reality by the Spirit of God. We are living witnesses that Spiritual Dating works when you understand how a citizen of the kingdom is supposed to live and position themselves to attract the mate of their soul.

- You do not have to go the way of the world just to find the right mate.
- You do not have to date one person after the other wasting time, energy and money trying to discover the right person for you.
- You do not have to get on one dating site after another trying to find the right hook-up.

There is a better reality and it is called Spiritual Dating for citizens of the Kingdom of God. I can testify that this works but I have not always known what I know today. There was a time when I (Dexter Jones) had the ideas of dating as mentioned above and because these things were the only realities that I knew I went on one date after another, wasted time, money and energy with people that I shouldn't have. I have even tried to help out God on more than one occasion to bring to me the mate of my soul. But one day God revealed to me what I now call Spiritual Dating for citizens of the Kingdom of God. With Spiritual Dating it doesn't take months and years for God to bring the right person into your life, he can do it in a matter of days. When you get the revelation of how to operate in the realm of the spirit you will not have to go looking, for God will bring that individual into your life. What would take you years just to find even someone that you will be happy settling with God will bring you not Mr. or Ms. Available but your Soul Mate and Life Mate in a matter of days, weeks or months, according to your faith it will be done unto you.

When I got the revelation of Spiritual Dating I was living in Orlando Fl and Petula was living in North Carolina. God begin to move upon me to move back to North Carolina however I was hesitant to do so because I felt like I would find my mate in Florida and this was where I wanted to live. However, through circumstances and situations I was forced to move back to North Carolina but before I left Florida I wrote down in my tablet that within 30 days I believe God to find my Soul Mate and Life Mate. I had begun to do Spiritual Dating by applying the things you will learn in this book.

That was on June 24, 2009, I wish I could tell you that it took 30 days to do this but I have a better testimony than that. I arrived in North Carolina on the 24th of June and one day later June 25, 2009 God brought my wife to me by orchestrating a scenario where the two of us came into contact with each other. We did not date for years because there was no need to prolong what God had done in the spirit realm in bringing us together. On July 17, 2010 we were walking down the aisles ready to say I do to each other and begin the journey of husband and wife one year and twenty three days later. We knew within two weeks after meeting each other that this was the Lord's doing without a shadow of a doubt and it was marvelous in our eyes.

We were two citizens of the kingdom desiring to find the man/woman of God that he had ordained for our lives. We were ready to take the next step into destiny knowing that this union was ordained of God and that he had purpose for bringing us together. As of this book he has blessed our lives tremendously and empowered us to be about the King's business in reaching out to help others on their journey. We have had tests on our journey but we realize that with every test comes a testimony and after the rain has subsided then comes the rainbow as a sign that our greater is coming. Currently in our work for the Lord he has blessed us to do various things such as:

- Being in ministry together with a call to reach out to singles.
- Become leaders over a singles ministry where we minister to singles monthly.
- Have a television broadcast where we reach out to singles to inspire and inform them on a bi-monthly basis in their singleness about the King's way to live and thrive as a single person.
- We have spoken at retreats, single gatherings, churches etc... fulfilling the mission that the King has called us to do from the foundation of the world.
- We have written over 10 books that deal with singles, singles caring for the things of God, single living, dating, relationships etc...
- And we're just getting started the best is yet to come; God has blessed us to do these things within the first two years of our marriage.

So we're here to tell you that yes Spiritual Dating works and that you don't have to settle in life with Mr. or Ms. Available and live with a person that will cause you much frustration in life. The King has a better plan and method for you to meet that man/woman of God that will be an asset to your life in every way possible. It's time for you to create your realities and in order to do that we present to you Kingdom Dating 1 — Spiritual Dating for Citizens of the Kingdom of God. Get ready to go on a spiritual journey of adventure and intrigue into the realm of the spirit where things are continually revealed and there is life more abundantly.

1
The King and the Kingdom

"Now after that John was put in prison, Jesus came into Galilee, preaching the gospel of the kingdom of God." Mark 1:14

This is a chapter that you will find in several of the books in the Kingdom Dating Series. This chapter is a repetition so that the Holy Spirit can enlighten your eyes to know the importance of your citizenship.

In order to understand kingdom dating we must first delve into the idea of who is King and what does the kingdom consist of. In the book of Matthew 2:2, we first hear of Jesus being called King in the scripture stating, *"Where is he that is born King of the Jews? for we have seen his star in the east, and are come to worship him."*

(Another instance we hear Jesus claiming himself as King saying, *"Then Pilate entered into the judgment hall again, and called Jesus, and said unto him, Art thou the King of the Jews? Jesus answered him, Sayest thou this thing of thyself, or did others tell it thee of me? Pilate answered, Am I a Jew? Thine own nation and the chief priest have delivered thee unto me: what hast thou done? Jesus answered, My kingdom is not of this world: if my kingdom were of this world, then would my servants fight, that I should not be delivered to the Jews: but now is my kingdom not from thence. Pilate therefore* said unto him, Art thou a king then? Jesus answered, Thou sayest that I am a king. **To this end was I born, and for this cause came I into the world, that I should bear witness unto the truth.** Every one that is of the truth heareth my voice." John 18:33-37

Here we see Jesus proclaiming himself as King and he has come forth to preach the gospel or good news of the kingdom. In his first message about the kingdom it says, "From that time Jesus began to preach, and to say, Repent: for the kingdom of heaven is at hand." Matthew 4:17 Jesus message was a proclamation to turn individuals from their ways and turn them to the ways of the kingdom. As a King he has come forth to proclaim his kingdom and invite all that will to come and partake of the kingdom.

His kingdom is not an earthly kingdom that you can see with the natural eye. It is not a visible kingdom that you can touch with your hands but it is a spiritual kingdom and you enter into it by faith through salvation. You cannot join it nor buy your way into it you must be born into it by way of the Spirit. You have already been born once by the birth of your parents but now you must be born from above.

Jesus told Nicodemus, "Verily, verily, I say unto thee, Except a man be born again, he cannot see the kingdom of God. Nicodemus saith unto him, How can a man be born when he is old? can he enter the second time into his mother's womb, and be born? Jesus answered,

Verily, verily, I say unto thee, Except a man be born of water and of the Spirit, he cannot enter into the kingdom of God. That which is born of the flesh is flesh; and that which is born of the Spirit is spirit. Marvel not that I said unto thee, Ye must be born again." John 3:3-7

The message of the King is plain and simple, you must be born again, and you must repent and turn from your ways and obey the ways of the kingdom. Except you be born again you cannot see, believe nor know the things of the kingdom because they are revealed to you by the Spirit of God. He that does not have the Spirit of God does not belong to God and cannot know the things of God. *"For what man knoweth the things of a man, save the spirit of man which is in him? even so the things of God knoweth no man, but the Spirit of God. Now we have received, not the spirit of the world, but the spirit which is of God; that we might know the things that are freely given to us of God. Which things also we speak, not in the words which man's wisdom teacheth, but which the Holy Ghost teacheth; comparing spiritual things with spiritual. But the natural man receiveth not the things of the Spirit of God: for they are foolishness unto him: neither can he know them, because they are spiritually discerned." 1 Corinthians 2:11-14*

As citizens of the kingdom you must know what the kingdom of God is and what it isn't. Another definition of the kingdom according to the Kings manual (the Bible) is that the kingdom is, *"righteousness, peace and joy in the Holy Ghost."Romans 14:17* In other words righteousness is the right standing that citizens has with the King that comes by acceptance of the King. Peace and joy in the Holy Ghost are the fruit of the Spirit that is given to all citizens of the kingdom. Those that are foreigners and aliens which are not a part of the kingdom desires these things but until they accept the King they will never have them. This is why a citizen cannot date a foreigner or alien, these individuals are contrary to the ways of the kingdom and do not possess the fruit of the kingdom.

In this book you will learn things that concern the kingdom about dating that will seem foolish to the natural man. All of your dating ideas that do not come from the Kings' manual (**the Bible**) are foolish in the eyes of the King. When your ideas are contrary to the ideas of the King and his kingdom you are a rebel and a disobedient person to the King.

The King has one main concern and that is his kingdom and the manual by which his kingdom is ran. The most important thing in the kingdom is the manual which consist of the words of the King. The kingdom is the sphere of God's sovereign rule and domain. Because the kingdom is not an earthly kingdom that can be seen naturally it is still as real as any earthly kingdom. However, it is revealed to those that accept the teaching of the King and obey his words. The kingdom is spiritual and cannot be seen by sight but by faith and if you can receive it by faith you will have no need of an observation of the kingdom.

The Pharisees in doubt asked Jesus about the kingdom saying, *"And when he was demanded of the Pharisees, when the kingdom of God should come, he answered them and said, The kingdom of God cometh not with observation (by sight and what you can see naturally): Neither shall they say, Lo here! or, lo there! for, behold, the kingdom of God is within you." Luke 17:20-21* When you accept the King you also have the kingdom for the King and his kingdom are one. When it says the kingdom of God is within you it means the King is in your midst and now that the King is your Lord and abides in you his rule and reign and all that he is and has is dwelling in your spirit man.

As a citizen of the kingdom you come under the rule of the King and follow the laws of the kingdom. Every citizen of the kingdom favors the King and his laws and daily abides by them. As citizens, *"Now therefore ye are no more strangers and foreigners, but fellow citizens with the saints, and of the household of God." Ephesians 2:19*

Your mission as a citizen is to learn the commandments and words from the manual of the King, *"And thou shalt love the LORD thy God (the King) with all thy heart, and with all thy soul, and with all thy mind, and with all thy strength: this is the first commandment. And the second is like, namely this, Thou shalt love thy neighbor as thyself. There is none other commandments greater than these. Mark 12:30-31*

As a citizen of the kingdom here are some of the things that you must do and know:

"But seek ye first the kingdom of God, and his righteousness; and all these things shall be added unto you." Matthew 6:33

"For the kingdom of God is not meat and drink; but righteousness, and peace, and joy in the Holy Ghost." Romans 14:17

"For the kingdom of God is not in word, but in power." 1 Corinthians 4:20

"Know ye not that the unrighteous shall not inherit the kingdom of God? Be not deceived: neither fornicators, nor idolaters, nor adulterers, nor effeminate, nor abusers of themselves with mankind, Nor thieves, nor covetous, nor drunkards, nor revilers, nor extortioners, shall inherit the kingdom of God." 1 Corinthians 6:9-10

"Who hath delivered us from the power of darkness, and hath translated us into the kingdom of his dear Son." Colossians 1:13

"And I will give unto thee the keys of the kingdom of heaven: and whatsoever thou shalt bind on earth, shall be bound in heaven: and whatsoever thou shalt loose on earth shall be loosed in heaven." Matthew 16:19

Herein is the message in its simplicity, if you obey the words of the King you are a child of the King and a citizen of the kingdom, *"And if children, then heirs; heirs of God, and joint heirs with Christ." Romans 8:17 "Fear not, little flock; for it is your Father's good pleasure to give you the kingdom."Luke 12:32*

2
The Natural Realm

"And so it is written, The first man Adam was made a living soul; the last Adam was made a quickening spirit. Howbeit that was not first which is spiritual, but that which is natural; and afterward that which is spiritual." 1 Corinthians 15:45-46

In life there is a natural realm and there is a spiritual realm. Most individuals live more in the natural realm than the spiritual realm. Operating in the natural realm alone can only provide for you natural things and cannot enable you to tap into the spiritual realm that is needed to give you the advantage in life. We actually live in a spiritual world and because we cannot see spiritual things mankind operates more by the natural realm than the spiritual realm he was designed for. Thereby limiting himself from the advantages he could have if he only learned that the spiritual realm is more real than the natural realm.

Once you learn how to operate in the spiritual realm you will then be able to move in the spiritual world and accomplish more in a day than you could accomplish in months operating by the natural realm alone. The majority of individuals are unable to meet their soul mate in life even though their soul mate at this very moment wants to know where they are and is ready to meet the person of their dreams. The natural realm is a more familiar realm because it's the realm that we can see, feel, touch, taste and smell. Most individuals live a lifetime in the natural realm and follow natural principles thereby walking by sight instead of by faith. However the scriptures *says "But the natural man receiveth not the things of the Spirit of God: for they are foolishness unto him: neither can he know them, for they are spiritually discerned."* 1 Corinthians 2:14

Because individuals don't know how to move in the spiritual realm and get that which rightly belongs to them they continually live beneath their privileges. In order to find the mate of your soul you must move beyond the natural because that realm will only bring you dates but not your soul mate. The natural realm will cause you to go by:

- The sight of your eyes.
- The hearing of your natural ears only.
- The feeling of your natural emotions only.

You can't live in the natural realm and expect to:

- See spiritual things.
- Hear spiritual things.
- And operate by spiritual discernment.

A good example of a natural man trying to understand spiritual things is the meeting of Jesus and Nicodemus. Jesus begins to tell him that he must be born again and Nicodemus ask *"How can a man be born when he is old? can he enter the second time into his mother's womb, and be born? Jesus answered and said unto him, Art thou a master of Israel, and knowest not these things? Verily, verily, I say unto thee, We speak that we do know, and testify that we have seen; and ye receive not our witness. If I have told you earthly (natural) things, and ye believe not, how shall ye believe if I tell you of heavenly (spiritual) things?" John 3:4, 10-12.*

The natural realm is where the world and carnal citizens learn how to meet their mates by following only natural principles that are supposed to be the answer for marital bliss. The natural realm is not where citizens of the kingdom meet their mates. In the natural realm you will go through one person after another trying to find Mr. or Ms. Right. Because you're not able to tap into the realm of the spirit like a true citizen of the kingdom you will rely totally on your wits, your intelligence and the sight of your eyes.

- In the natural realm is the lust of the eyes.
- In the natural realm is the lust of the flesh.
- In the natural realm is the pride of life.
- In the natural realm is carnality.
- In the natural realm is spiritual death.

As long as you live by the natural you will not

find a virtuous woman because a truly virtuous woman is a spiritual woman. It takes God to bring you a virtuous woman and he will not bring a virtuous woman to a natural or carnal man. The scripture ask a question, *"Who can find a virtuous woman?" Proverbs 31:10a* The answer is obvious; no one because her value is to high *"for her price is far above rubies." Proverbs 31:10b* It takes God to find such a woman and God is a Spirit and he only operates in the spiritual realm.

As long as you live by the natural realm you will never find a faithful man because a truly faithful man is a spiritual man. It takes God to bring you to a faithful man and he will not bring a natural or carnal woman to a faithful man. The scripture ask a question here also saying, *"Who can find a faithful man?" Proverbs 20:6* The answer is obvious; no one because faithfulness is a fruit of the Spirit and only a spiritual man from God can fill those shoes.

When you live by the natural realm you will slow your progress of finding your soul mate by at least 80%. And when you live by the natural you will often live a life of doubt, unbelief, fear and uncertainty. Fear creates for you a magnetic field that pulls to you the things you fear and where fear is you will not attract to you your soul mate but just more dates.

3
The Spirit of Fear

"For God hath not given us the spirit of fear; but of power, and of love, and of a sound mind." 2 Timothy 2:7

Either you're living your life in faith or you're living it in fear. Most people are living in fear and they're attracting the things which they fear instead of the things they truly desire. Fear is a spirit and the objective of that spirit is to cause anxiety, cause you to be afraid, panic, trepidation, uncertainty, unbelief and distrust. You cannot operate in faith and fear at the same time, one or the other has the preeminence in your life and is attracting to you your present relationship status.

- Fear is belief in the seen.
- Fear is belief in the natural.
- Fear is belief in the negative.
- Fear will paralyze you from operating in the unseen realm.
- Fear is limiting and bondage.

Fear creates a magnetic field that pulls to you the things you fear. In the book of Job he stated, *"For the thing which I greatly feared is come upon me and that which I was afraid of is come unto me." Job 3:25* As a single citizen of the kingdom that desire to be married you must get rid of fear and replace it with faith. When you say such things as:

- It's hard to find the right man/woman in life.
- All the good men/women are taken.
- I wonder will I ever get married.
- Why is it so hard to find Mr. or Ms. Right?
- It seems like God is not hearing me.

When you say such things you are living in fear and are being overtaken by a spirit that causes you to be uncertain about your relationship future. A spirit that causes anxiety in your life and distrust in your Creator who says, *"But seek ye first the kingdom of God and his righteousness and all these things shall be added unto you." Matthew 6:33*

Also when fear has the preeminence in your life it shows that you're not walking in perfect love for *"There is no fear in love; but perfect love casteth out fear: because fear hath torment. He that feareth is not made perfect in love." 1 John 4:18* The definition of torment means to have extreme pain, anguish, torture, misery, vexation and distress. How are you going to attract your soul mate with all these emotions going on in your heart and mind? The answer is you're not going to attract the right person but just individuals that will fill that empty space in your life but not the empty space in your heart. That space is designed for your Soul Mate to fill. When God created Adam he knew that Adam needed a companion so he made Eve for Adam.

Likewise God has just the right person for you that will compliment you in every way, but you must get rid of fear and learn to move in the realm of the spirit where faith lives and your Soul Mate abides.

4
The Spirit Realm

"If I have told you earthly things, and ye believe not, how shall ye believe, if I tell you of heavenly (spiritual) things." John 3:12

Just as there is a natural realm there is also a spiritual realm. If you want to connect with the mate of your soul then you must do it in the spirit realm. The natural realm will only bring you more dates but not your soul mate. The spiritual realm will always bring you your soul mate. When you learn how to operate in the spiritual realm you can accomplish more in a day than others will accomplish in months.

- The spirit world is more real than the natural world.
- The natural world is the seen world and the temporal.
- The spirit world is the unseen world and the eternal.
- The natural world is the world that mankind is more familiar with and therefore the world we operate by basically all of our life.
- The spiritual world is the unfamiliar world and the world to mankind that is shrouded in darkness, secrecy and the unknown.

If we could actually understand these two worlds as God would have us to we would see that;

- The natural world is like night.
- The spiritual world is like day.
- The natural world is limited.
- The spiritual world is unlimited.
- In the natural world we look for our soul mate like everyone else.
- In the spiritual world we use the spiritual realm and spiritual laws to call our soul mate forth.
- In the natural world we walk by sight.
- In the spiritual world we walk by faith and see through the eyes of the spirit.
- In the natural world we think like a natural man.
- In the spiritual world we think like God.

If you try to find your soul mate using natural world methods only you may never find them, they may evade you on every turn and continue to be out of your grasp and reach. The soul mate you're seeking is the one that can bring out the best in you, the one that can inspire you to be all you can be, the one that motivates you to take life more serious than ever before and the one that God uses to bring about a change in your life. Because this individual is so good for you and "*every good and perfect thing come from above"* the adversary and enemy of your soul will do everything in his power to keep the two of you apart. Your enemy Satan the devil doesn't want your soul mate and you to come together because he knows what a powerhouse the two of you can be.

So he makes it his business to bring the wrong person before you to entice you into thinking that this person is your soul mate and life mate. While all the time it's nothing but Satan that is appearing **"as an angel of light",** to throw both of you off your course from meeting the one that's supposed to be your true soul mate.

The person he brings before you isn't compatible with you yet we allow our emotions to be stirred up and begin to walk more by sight and feelings than by faith and an inner knowing that never fails to produce truth and exact knowledge. We have failed the test and our adversary has tricked us and now wants to devour us in the midst of a bad relationship and marriage. I have told my soul mate over and over that she was born for me and I likewise was born for her, we're for each other.

The scriptures warn us of our adversary that operates in the spirit world while we operate in the natural world with no weapons to fight and foresee his tact and wiles. Saying, *"Be sober, be viligant; because your adversary the devil, as a roaring lion, walketh about, seeking whom he may devour: Whom resist steadfast in the faith, knowing that the same afflictions are accomplished in your brethern in the world." 1 Peter 5:8-9 "Put on the whole armour of God, that ye may be able to stand against the wiles of the devil. For we wrestle not against flesh and blood, but against (the spirit world) principalities, powers, against the rulers of the darkness of this world, against spiritual wickedness in high places. Wherefore take unto you, the whole armour of God, that ye may be able to withstand in the evil day, and having done all, to stand. Stand therefore, having your loins girt about with truth,and having on the breastplate of righteousness. And your feet shod with the preparation of the gospel of peace; Above all, taking the shield of faith, wherewith ye shall be able to quench all the fiery darts of the wicked. And take the helmet of salvation and the sword of the Spirit, which is the word of God: Praying always with all prayer and supplication in the Spirit, and watching thereunto with all perseverance and supplication for all saints." Ephesians 6:11-18*

These are the spiritual weapons we need to fight in the spirit world because our adversary is a spiritual being and we cannot fight him by natural means and with natural weapons. As we put on the whole armour of God we will be equipped to see, hear, think and operate in the spirit realm using spiritual laws to give us the advantage so that we will not be ignorant of Satan devices nor of operating in the spirit world.

The Spirit Realm vs. The Natural Realm

"But the natural man receiveth not the things of the Spirit of God: for they are foolishness unto him: neither can he know them, because they are spiritually discerned." 1 Corinthians 2:14 In this world you have the natural man that operates and lives by the natural realm and you have the spiritual man that operates and lives by the spirit realm. The natural man cannot operate and live by the spirit realm nor does he receive the things of the Spirit for they are foolishness to him and he cannot understand the spirit realm or spiritual things.

To give you an example of how the natural works when it try to operate by the spirit. It would be like taking a child and sitting him in the seat of the top fortune 500 companies and ask the child to run it with what knowledge they have, impossible. They will be completely lost without a clue of what to do because such a task is just too much for them to handle, their little minds have not been equipped to handle such broad and detailed administrative work.

Because most individuals operate mainly in the natural realm of life they have no idea of the power and ability that the spirit realm holds, no idea that what they're struggling with in the natural can be easily conquered in the spirit. The majority of individuals in the world aren't in relationships or married to their soul mates, most people are in relationships and marriages that they are simply enduring and putting up with.

They don't have a complete and happy relationship or marriage and the divorce rate proves this point, when you have one out of two marriages ending in divorce it is evident that we have a problem and it's getting worse all the time.

- Individuals don't have a clue of how to find the individual that is good for them. 1 Corinthians 2:15
- Individuals don't have a clue of how to discern in the spirit. 1 Corinthians 2:14
- Individuals don't have a clue of how to be led of the spirit so they will not fulfill the lust of the flesh. Galatians 5:16-17
- Individuals don't have a clue of how to compare spiritual things with spiritual. 1 Corinthians 2:13
- Individuals don't have a clue of how to call forth their soul mate in the spirit realm. Job 22:28

It is true that we live in a natural world and we operate in many things by natural means but there are some things that we can do by spiritual means in this natural world and see results 80% quicker. When we learn how and when to operate spiritually in this natural realm we will be able to cut our efforts in more than half the time and see progress and success more expedient than the natural man working by the natural realm only.

As an example let us behold some instances of Jesus living in this natural realm but operating by the spirit realm. "*And it came to pass, as the people pressed upon him to hear the word of God, he stood by the lake of Gennesaret, And saw two ships standing by the lake: but the fishermen were gone out of them, and were washing their nets. And he entered into one of the ships, which was Simon's, and prayed him that he would thrust out a little from the land. And he sat down, and taught the people out of the ship. Now when he had left speaking, he said unto Simon, Launch out into the deep, and let down your nets for a draught. And Simon (a professional fisherman fishing by totally natural means in the natural world) said unto him, Master we have toiled all the night, and have taken nothing: nevertheless at thy word I will let down the net. (They saw nothing Jesus operating in the spirit realm saw a multitude). And when they had done this, they inclosed a great multitude of fishes: and their net brake. And they beckoned unto their partners, which were in the other ship, that they should come and help them. And they came, and filled both the ships, so that they began to sink. When Simon Peter saw it, he fell down at Jesus' knees, saying Depart from me; for I am a sinful man, O Lord. **For he was astonished,** and all that were with him, at the drought of the fishes which they had taken.*" St. Luke 5:1-9

Peter and his partners were professional fishermen and they had toiled all night and had not caught anything, no doubt they knew the best spots and had the best natural equipment for fishing but they did not know how to operate in the spirit realm when the natural realm fail to produce.

But Jesus knew how to operate in the natural and spirit realm and knew where to locate the fishes and what they needed to use to catch the multitudes. If you will notice the scriptures said he told Simon to let down their nets meaning more than one net for a draught but instead Simon only let down the net meaning one net and as a result the net brake. If he would have did as Jesus said and let down his nets it would have been enough to hold his catch for Jesus did not come to destroy his equipment but to be a blessing to him for allowing him to use his boat.

Another example of Jesus living in the natural realm but operating in the spirit realm when the time was needed is the wedding in Cana. *"And the third day there was a marriage in Cana of Galilee; and the mother of Jesus was there: And both Jesus was called, and his disciples, to the marriage. And when they wanted wine, the mother of Jesus saith unto him, They have no wine. Jesus saith unto her, Woman, what have I to do with thee? mine hour is not yet come. His mother saith unto the servants, Whatsoever he saith unto you, do it. And there were set there six waterpots of stone, after the manner of the purifying of the Jews, containing two or three firkins apiece. Jesus saith unto them, Fill the waterpots with water. And they filled them to the brim. And he saith unto them, Draw out now, and bear unto the governor of the feast. And they bare it. When the ruler of the feast had tasted the water that was made wine, and knew not whence it was: (but the servants which drew the water knew;) the governor of the feast called the bridegroom, And saith unto him, Every man at the beginning doth set forth the good wine; and when men have well drunk, then that which is worse: but thou hast kept the good wine until now. This beginning of miracles did Jesus in Cana of Galilee, and manifested forth his glory; and his disciples believed on him." St. John 2:1-11*

The bridegroom was in a predicament he had run out of wine and did not have any more to furnish for his guests, he should have made sure there was enough wine on hand to last throughout the wedding but lo this situation has now arisen and they didn't know what to do. So the mother of Jesus steps in and tells him *"They have no wine"* but Jesus did not want to necessarily perform this miracle for he said *"Woman, what have I to do with thee? mine hour is not yet come."* Nevertheless he did it; the bridegroom no doubt was at his wits end for to run out of wine was a bad thing. But Jesus knowing how to operate in the natural and spirit realm knew what to do to produce more wine.

He moved in the realm of the spirit which always exceeds the natural realm and produced wine out of water and the wedding was a success because one man understood the spirit realm and how to operate in it. What does all this have to do with finding your soul mate you may ask? If you don't operate in the spirit realm where there are no impossibilities you will not find your soul mate by operating in the natural realm. You will end up being a statistic in the divorce section or at best enduring a relationship or marriage.

Not many people find their soul mate in life because not many know how to find them and as a result individuals end up settling for less than the best for their life. But if you learn how to operate in the spirit realm and apply spiritual laws you will most certainly find your soul mate and enjoy the celebration of love that God has ordained for your life.

Spiritual Laws vs. Natural Laws

"It is the spirit that quickeneth; the flesh profiteth nothing: the words that I speak unto you, they are spirit, and they are life." St. John 6:63 There are natural laws and there are spiritual laws, the natural have its order of operation and so does the spiritual. Both laws are understood and represented by words the words of these laws explain to us what they are and what we must do in order to obey them and receive the greatest benefit.

If we fail to obey the natural laws we must suffer the consequences of our disobedience, these natural laws have no respect of person and they will produce for you or fail to produce for you according to your obedience or disobedience. In the natural world one law we will observe is the law of gravity, now this is just a natural law yet it works the same for all mankind, it doesn't matter what your last name is, your position or status in life the law of gravity is the same for all.

If a rich man on Wall Street were to jump off a tall building the law of gravity will immediately go into effect for him and will draw him downward to the ground "for what goes up must come down." If the bum on the street were to jump off a tall building the law of gravity will immediately go into effect for him and will likewise draw him downward to the ground "for what goes up must come down." It's a law that's a law that's a law that's a law. It works the same for all mankind and will not change no matter who you are or what you possess naturally. As long as you live in this natural world and operate in the natural realm you will live and die in your relationship life by these natural laws unless God chooses to supersede these natural laws in your behalf you are destined for the natural.

Let's observe what the scriptures say about the natural as well as the spiritual and then we will show you how it all ties in with using spiritual laws to call forth your soul mate. The natural is weak in comparison to the spiritual, as we observe our natural bodies there are laws that govern this natural body and the ultimate law says that this body shall return to the dust from whence it came. But the ultimate spiritual law in reference to the body says it shall be resurrected in power.

- The spiritual law always outweighs the natural laws and is able to do far more than any natural law at any time.

- The spiritual law is like dynamite while the natural law in comparison is like a firecracker.

- The spiritual law is like the atomic boom while the natural law is like the h-boom.

So says the scriptures; *"So also is the resurrection of the dead. It is sown in corruption, it is raised in incorruption. It is sown in dishonour; it is raised in glory: it is sown in weakness; it is raised in power: It is sown a natural body; it is raised a spiritual body. There is a natural body, and there is a spiritual body. And so it is written. The first man Adam was made a living soul; the last Adam was made a quickening spirit. Howbeit that was not first which is spiritual, but that which is natural; and afterward that which is spiritual. The first man is of the earth, earthy: the second man is the Lord from heaven. As is the earthy, such are they also that are earthy: as is the heavenly, such are they also that are heavenly. As we have borne the image of the earthy, we shall also bear the image of the heavenly."* 1 Corinthians 15:42-49

As you can see the spiritual and heavenly outweighs the natural and earthy. It is the same when natural laws come up against spiritual laws there is no comparison; yet we will observe a natural law at work in comparison to a spiritual law in the same work.

Natural laws = Jesus disciples had gotten into the ship in order to go to the other side of the sea, this is a natural thing, you get in a natural man made ship to cross the sea and the ship floats on the water to get them to the other side, so it goes; *"And when evening was come, the ship was in the midst of the sea, tossed with waves, and he (Jesus) alone on the land. And he saw them toiling in rowing for the wind was contrary unto them."* Mark 6:47-48a, Matthew 14:24

Natural laws = Here we have an example of natural men doing natural things in order to get natural results yet the natural things they're doing are not able to handle this occurrence of the stormy weather. So they continually try to bring things under control by natural means but they're unable to do it. When such storms occur out of the ordinary most times there is a force behind these occurrences. It will either take God's mercy on your behalf or a (spiritual man or woman) that knows how to operate in the spirit world, tapping the spirit realm and using spiritual laws to supersede the natural.

Spiritual laws = Now Jesus had sent the multitude away and *afterwards "he went up into a mountain apart to pray: and when evening was come, he was there alone. And in the fourth watch of the night Jesus went unto them, walking on the sea, and would have passed by them. But when they saw him walking upon the sea, they supposed it had been a spirit, and cried out: For they all saw him, and were troubled. And immediately he talked with them, and saith unto them, Be of good cheer: it is I be not afraid. And he went up into the ship; and the wind ceased: and they were sore amazed in themselves beyond measure, and wondered." Mark 6:48-51, Matthew 14:23-26*

Spiritual laws = Here we have Jesus a spiritual man operating in the spirit world using the spirit realm and working by spiritual laws has come upon the disciples in the ship tossed with waves and the wind was contrary. Unlike the disciples he did not fear and his presence alone caused the wind to cease. Here is Jesus superseding natural laws with spiritual laws, he walks on water while the disciples go by ship. When he gets into the ship the wind ceased while the disciples frantically tries to get control of the ship by rowing and steering it to safety. Jesus is operating totally by spiritual laws and the disciples are operating totally by natural laws and again the spiritual excels the natural.

Yet lo and behold we have an incident that occurs that causes a natural man to try and operate by the spirit world moving in the spirit realm and operating by spiritual laws, and lo and behold it works. So it goes, "*And Peter answered him and said, Lord, if it be thou, bid me come unto thee on the water (now Peter wants to walk on water) And he said, Come. And when Peter was come down out of the ship, HE WALKED ON THE WATER, to go to Jesus. But when he saw the wind boisterous, he was afraid; and beginning to sink, he cried, saying, Lord, save me. And immediately Jesus stretched forth his hand and caught him and said unto him, O thou of little faith, wherefore didst thou doubt.*" St. Matthew 14:28-31

Here we see that natural man through Christ can operate in the spirit world moving in the spirit realm and use spiritual laws to supersede natural laws.

- The key to it all is that first Peter asked Jesus if he could come on the water.
- Second, Jesus tells Peter to come on the water.
- Third, as a result of Peter's obedience to the word of Jesus he is able to do the impossible and walk on water.
- Fourth, Peter begins to observe the circumstances and situation.

- Fifth, he stops operating in the spirit world and begins to operate in the natural world. He gets out of the spirit realm and begins to move by the natural realm where fear instead of faith is more dominant. As a result he becomes afraid.
- Sixth, he no longer operates by spiritual laws but begin to focus on natural laws and the natural law says man cannot walk on water and the law of gravity which was suspended now comes back into action and as a result he begins to sink.

The reason that Peter begins to sink is because he focuses once again on the natural law of life and in the natural fear reigns and doubt is right behind it, this forfeits faith which operates by spiritual laws. And Jesus says to him *"O thou of little faith, wherefore didst thou doubt." Matthew 14:28-31* His fear and doubt caused him to sink when before he was actually walking on water just like Jesus was. So we see that the spiritual laws can be tapped by anyone that will obey God and do according to his word.

Operating in the natural laws of life may never help you find your soul mate; multitudes have lived and died having never found the person of their dreams when they could have if they only knew how to operate by spiritual laws.

- Spiritual laws can do the impossible.

- Spiritual laws will prevail where all natural laws have failed.
- Spiritual laws will enable you to step out of the ship while everyone else stays in the ship.
- Spiritual laws will bring forth your soul mate when before you were only able to get just dates.
- Spiritual laws can break through every barrier and suspend natural laws long enough to give you a breakthrough.

If you want God to bring your soul mate and you together you must begin to operate by the spiritual laws that aren't hindered by time or space. The key to using spiritual laws is having faith that the thing which you desire and requesting shall happen without a shadow of a doubt. A spiritual law is nothing more than a spiritual pattern or principle of doing things and that law does not change for anyone or anything. The spiritual law of relationship is the law of attraction, the law of sowing and reaping, the law of cause and effect and it's all based on the premise of faith and belief.

- You must believe that what you're asking for you shall receive.
- You must believe that your request is not impossible but possible.

- You must have faith in God or the God kind of faith.
- You must say to your situation of singleness, *"Be thou removed, and be thou cast into the sea."* *Mark 11:23*
- You must not doubt in your heart or spirit.
- You must believe that those things which you said shall come to pass.
- You must believe that you shall have that very thing which you have spoken.
- You must know that your request is the perfect will of God.
- You must know that God wants you to find your soul mate.
- You must know that when you asked God to bring your soul mate and you together he had already begin to set the whole thing into motion.
- You must know that this is by faith and not by sight.
- You must know that you're operating by the spirit world and God is on your side and for you.
- You must know that you're moving in the spirit realm which is not limited by time, distance or space.
- You must know that you're operating by spiritual laws that is greater than natural laws

and can supersede them at any time to bring your objective to pass.

You must believe and know that what things you ask you shall certainly receive them.

5
Spiritual Dating

"Who against hope believed in hope, that he might become the father of many nations, according to that which was spoken, So shall they seed be." Romans 4:18

This chapter is the apex of all the other chapters in that it will reveal the concept of Spiritual Dating. Spiritual Dating is not like earthly dating in the sense that you work from natural principles to cause things to happen on your behalf. This is such a tough chapter to write because it is totally a spiritual chapter and is designed to take you behind the veil of the spirit and show you spiritual realities that only a spiritual person can truly receive. The manual speaks of it in this manner, *"Which things also we speak not in the words which man's wisdom teacheth, but which the Holy Ghost teacheth; comparing spiritual things with spiritual. But the natural man receiveth not the things of the Spirit of God: for they are foolishness unto him: neither can he know them, because they are **spiritually discerned.** But he that is spiritual judgeth all things, yet he himself is judged of no man. For who hath known the mind of the Lord, that he may instruct him? But we have the mind of Christ." 1 Corinthians 2:13-16*

Spiritual Dating is a concept that you rarely if ever hear of when it comes to dating and relationship because most individuals have not heard of it. It is such a rare truth that when it is first heard of it is almost unbelievable even to the spiritual minded citizen. However, you have to ask God to help you to understand this concept because it is through this understanding that you will learn how to meet your Soul Mate and Life Mate. Spiritual Dating will seem foolish to the natural mind and even the carnal minded citizen. But the manual says, *"Because the foolishness of God is wiser than men; and the weakness of God is stronger than men." 1 Corinthians 1:25*

There are not many people in life that have found their Soul Mate and Life Mate. We see this as we consider the divorce rate in the land with 1 out of 2 marriages ending in divorce and even some others that stay together for other reasons besides true love. Through Spiritual Dating God has chosen the:

- Foolish things of the world to confound the wise.
- Weak things of the world to confound the mighty.
- Base things of the world.
- Things which are despised.
- Things which are not.

In the words of the manual, *"But God hath chosen the foolish things of the world to confound the wise; and God hath chosen the weak things of the world to confound the mighty; And base things of the world, and things which are despised, hath God chosen, yea, and things which are not, to bring to nought things that are: That no flesh should glory in his presence. But of him are ye in Christ Jesus, who of God is made unto us wisdom, and righteousness, and sanctification, and redemption: That, according as it is written, He that glorieth, let him glory in the Lord." 1 Corinthians 1:27-31*

The whole concept of Spiritual Dating is that it is done in a manner that you cannot boast of but you will only be able to give God the glory for what he has done. Through Spiritual Dating you cannot arrange to meet your Soul Mate in the natural realm because the natural cannot produce them.

- In Earthly Dating you call up the individual to set up a date.
- In Spiritual Dating you call up God to set you up with a date.
- In Earthly Dating you pick by the sight of your eyes the date to go out with.
- In Spiritual Dating it's a blind date because you don't know who God has chosen for you.
- In Earthly Dating it's all natural dating just like the world dates.
- In Spiritual Dating its first spiritual and then you use Kingdom dating principles as a citizen of the Kingdom.
- Earthly Dating is like dating someone in the dark, you can't really see who you're dating.

- Spiritual Dating is like having on night goggles and you can see in the dark just as if it was light.

Spiritual Dating is faith dating because faith is a spiritual tool that can only be used by spiritual people. Faith is of the spirit and the manner in which it operates is by moving in the unseen realm where everything exists already and everything is already fulfilled. The manual says, *"Blessed be the God and Father of our Lord Jesus Christ, who hath blessed us (this is past tense) with all spiritual blessings in heavenly places in Christ."* Ephesians 1:3 The mate that you're seeking already exists in the spirit realm and the King knows who they are and where they are. Before something manifest in the natural realm it exists already in the spirit realm.

Therefore the way to date is to go in the spirit realm where the King abides and ask the King to direct and order the steps of the citizen of the Kingdom that he knows is best for you. When the King does something he calls the thing from the end to the beginning and manifests it in the present. When the King told Abram that he would have a son his wife Sarah laughed because she knew in the natural it was impossible to happen. So the story goes, *"And they said unto him, Where is Sarah they wife? And he said, Behold, in the tent. And he said, I will certainly return unto thee according to the time of life;*

and, lo, Sarah they wife shall have a son. And Sarah heard it in the tent door, which was behind him. Now Abraham and Sarah were old and well stricken in age; and it ceased to be with Sarah after the manner of women. Therefore Sarah laughed within herself, saying After I am waxed old shall I have pleasure, my lord being old also? And the LORD said unto Abraham, Wherefore did Sarah laugh, saying, Shall I of a surety bear a child, which am old? Is any thing too hard for the LORD? At the time appointed I will return unto thee, according to the time of life, and Sarah shall have a son. Then Sarah denied, saying, I laughed not; for she was afraid. And he said, Nay; but thou didst laugh." Genesis 18:9-15

You may have been single for 5, 10, 20 years or more but you must know that nothing is too hard for the King. What may seem an impossible situation for you is just right for the King? Through Spiritual Dating you don't look at your situation like the world looks at theirs but you must see it through the eyes of God. It is said that Abraham, *"Who against hope believed in hope (when you see no hope of potential prospects you must still have faith in the King that there are prospects and the King knows where they are) that he might become the father of many nations, according to that which was spoken, So shall they seed be." Romans 4:18*

In Spiritual Dating you seek the King and not the mate because the mate doesn't know who you are or where you are. The King knows where you both reside and who you both are and he knows how to orchestra a scenario to bring the both of you together. When you seek the King he will lead you and guide you either by word, circumstance or situation to get you into the right place you need to be to meet the mate of your soul. The manual said in reference to Abraham believing against hope, *"according to that which was spoken." Romans 4:18b* So the King in his wisdom knows how to speak a word to you that will give you direction to position you to be in the right place at the right time.

The key to receiving in Spiritual Dating is being strong in faith and believing the report of the King. The manual says, *"And (Abraham) being not weak in faith, he considered not his own body now dead (you may think that your relationship life has been dead but you must no longer consider it dead but alive from the dead) when he was about an hundred years old (you may have been single for 5, 10, 20, 30 years or more), neither yet the deadness of Sarah's womb. He staggered not at the promise of God through unbelief (you must not waver through unbelief at the word of the King when he speaks to you that this is your time) but was strong in faith (you must be strong in faith) giving glory to God; And being fully persuaded that, what he had promised, he was able also to perform.*

Spiritual Dating has more to do with believing for your Soul Mate and Life Mate than it does with praying continually for them. It does not say that Abraham spent a lot of time in prayer praying for a child but it says that **he believed God and was strong in faith.** *"And therefore it was imputed to him for righteousness. Now it was not written for his sake alone, that it was imputed to him; But for us also, to whom it shall be imputed, if we believe."* Romans 4:22-24a

As a citizen of the Kingdom you have been give a measure of faith and have been reckoned as children of Abraham. *"Even as Abraham believed God, and it was accounted to him for righteousness. Know ye therefore that they which are of faith, the same are the children of Abraham. So then they which be of faith are blessed with faithful Abraham."* Galatians 3:6-7, 9

There are far too many citizens of the Kingdom that don't know how to attract their Soul Mate and Life Mate. Spiritual Dating is the answer because it takes the pressure off of you to find that individual and puts it on the King to find them for you. The King in his Omniscience wisdom, Omnipotent power and Omnipresence Spirit knows all, is all powerful and is everywhere. In the beginning the King instituted marriage and brought the first couple together. Genesis 2:21-25 Still today the King says, *"Marriage is honourable in all."* Hebrews 13:4 That is an awesome word within itself to let you know that the King approves of marriage and that he wants you to be married if that's what you desire.

However, he doesn't stop there but says, *"For I would that all men were even as myself. But every man hath his proper gift of God, one after this manner, and another after that. I say therefore to the unmarried and widows, It is good for them if they abide even as I. But if they cannot contain let them marry: for it is better to marry than to burn. But and if thou marry, thou hast not sinned; and if a virgin marry, she hath not sinned. Nevertheless such shall have trouble in the flesh, but I spare you. So then he that giveth her in marriage doeth well." 1 Corinthians 7:7-9, 28, 38a*

The King want you to know that if you want to marry it is well, you are not less spiritual if you marry nor are you more spiritual if you don't marry. Marriage is an honorable thing and its God ordained. Marriage should never be taken likely nor be entered into inadvisably but you should look forward to marriage and realize that marriage begins in the dating stage. If you get it right in the dating stage you will have a blessed and prosperous marriage that will cause you to rejoice with your spouse. You will not have a marriage that you regret but a marriage that you will be proud of. The divorce rate is so high even among Christians because we have not been taught how to date and who to date and divorce has simply been the inevitable result of wrong dating and earthly dating.

In spiritual dating you don't date like the world date. Spiritual dating takes you beyond the natural and the seen.

- Natural dating ask others only what they

think about the person.

- Spiritual dating go straight to God and let God inform them about the person.
- Natural dating only sees the outward situation and what surrounds the person.
- Spiritual dating does like Elijah with his servant and says Lord open my eyes that I may see the real situation and surrounding of this person. 2 Kings
- Natural dating move quickly with no real witness or peace in their heart about the person.
- Spiritual dating asks God for a witness as Gideon did because they don't want to make a mistake and desire guidance from God. Judges 6:36-40
- Natural dating is afraid of real truth and what it may reveal.
- Spiritual dating wants to know the truth because it knows the truth will make you free and free indeed.

When you spiritual date you will know that the whole set up is by God and it is an amazing act and could have only been orchestrated by the Almighty himself. Your thought and conclusion of the matter will be as the Psalmist stated in Psalm 118:23 *"This is the LORD'S doing; it is marvellous in our eyes."*

6
Faith

"Through faith we understand that the worlds were framed by the word of God, so that things which are seen were not made of things which do appear." Hebrews 11:3

Faith is the opposite of fear. Either you're living your life from faith or you're living it from fear. In order to attract your Soul Mate and Life Mate you must begin to live a life of faith. Faith is of the spirit and it operates in the unseen realm because the things which are seen were not made of things which do appear. Because you cannot mix fear and faith together either fear or faith is having the preeminence in your relationship life at this very moment and our objective through this book is to get rid of fear and live by faith.

- Faith is belief in the unseen.
- Faith is belief in the spiritual.
- Faith is belief in the positive.
- Faith will cause you to operate in the unseen realm.
- Faith is unlimited and liberty.

Faith creates a magnetic field that pulls to you the things you believe for. In the book of Hebrew we have a list of the heroes of faith that obtained a good report as a result of their faith. It says, *"For by it the elders obtained a good report. Through faith we understand that the worlds were framed by the word of God, so that things which are seen were not made of things which do appear. By faith Abel offered unto God a more excellent sacrifice than Cain, by which he obtained witness that he was righteous, God testifying of his gifts: and by it he being dead yet speaketh. By faith Enoch was translated that he should not see death; and was not found, because God had translated him: for before his translation he had this testimony, that he pleased God. But without faith it is impossible to please him: for he that cometh to God must believe that he is, and that he is a rewarder of them that diligently seek him.*

By faith Noah, being warned of God of things not seen as yet, moved with fear, prepared an ark to the saving of his house; by the which he condemned the world, and became heir of the righteousness which is by faith. By faith Abraham, when he was called to go out into a place which he should after receive for an inheritance, obeyed; and he went out, not knowing whither he went. By faith he sojourned in the land of promise, as in a strange country, dwelling in tabernacles with Isaac and Jacob, the heirs with him of the same promise: For he looked for a city which hath foundations, whose builder and maker is God. Through faith also Sara herself received strength to conceive seed, and was delivered of a child when she was past age, because she judged him faithful who had promis-

ed. By faith Abraham, when he was tried, offered up Isaac: and he that had received the promises offered up his only begotten son, Of whom it was said, That in Isaac shall thy seed be called: Accounting that God was able to raise him up, even from the dead; from whence also he received him in a figure. By faith Isaac blessed Jacob and Esau concerning things to come. By faith Jacob, when he was a dying, blessed both the sons of Joseph; and worshipped, leaning upon the top of his staff. By faith Joseph, when he died, made mention of the departing of the children of Israel; and gave commandment concerning his bones.

By faith Moses, when he was born, was hid three months of his parents, because they saw he was a proper child; and they were not afraid of the king's commandment. By faith Moses, when he was come to years, refused to be called the son of Pharaoh's daughter; Choosing rather to suffer affliction with the people of God, than to enjoy the pleasures of sin for a season; Esteeming the reproach of Christ greater riches than the treasures in Egypt: for he had respect unto the recompence of the reward. By faith he forsook Egypt, not fearing the wrath of the king: for he endured, as seeing him who is invisible. Through faith he kept the passover, and the sprinkling of blood, lest he that destroyed the firstborn should touch them. By faith they passed through the Red sea as by dry land: which the Egyptians assaying to do were drowned. By faith the walls of Jericho fell down, after they were compassed about seven days. By faith the harlot Rahab perished not with them that believed not, when she had received the spies with peace. And what shall I more say? for the time would fail me to tell of Gedeon, and of Barak, and of Samson, and of Jephthae; of David also, and Samuel, and of the prophets: Who through faith subdued kingdoms, wrought righteousness, obtained promises, stopped the mouths of lions. Quenched the violence of fire, escaped the edge of the sword, out of weakness were made strong, waxed valiant in fight, turned to flight the armies of the aliens. Women received their dead raised to life again:" Hebrews 11:2-9, 17-35a

As a single citizen of the kingdom that desire to be married you must get rid of fear and replace it with faith. When you say such things as:

- It's hard to find the right man/woman in life.
- All the good men/women are taken.
- I wonder will I ever get married.
- Why is it so hard to find Mr. or Ms. Right?
- It seems like God is not hearing me.

When you say such things you are living in fear and are being overtaken by a spirit that causes you to be uncertain about your future. A spirit that causes anxiety in your life and distrust in your Creator who says, *"But seek ye first the kingdom of God and his righteousness and all these things shall be added unto you." Matthew 6:33*

Also when fear has the preeminence in your life it shows that you're not walking in perfect love for

"There is no fear in love; but perfect love casteth out fear: because fear hath torment. He that feareth is not made perfect in love." 1 John 4:18 The definition of torment means to have extreme pain, anguish, torture, misery, vexation and distress. How are you going to attract your soul mate with all these emotions going on in your heart and mind? The answer is you're not going to attract the right person but just individuals that will fill that empty space in your life but not the empty space in your heart. That space is designed for your Soul Mate to fill. When God created Adam he knew that Adam needed a companion so he made Eve for Adam.

Likewise God has just the right person for you that will compliment you in every way, but you must get rid of fear and learn to move in the realm of the spirit where your Soul Mate abides. For *"He is able to do exceeding abundantly above all we ask or think according to the power that worketh in us."* Ephesians 3:20

7
Spiritual Thinking

"Finally, brethren, whatsoever things are true, whatsoever things are honest, whatsoever things are just, whatsoever things are pure, whatsoever things are lovely, whatsoever things are of good report; if there be any virtue; if there be any praise, think on these things."
Philippians 4:8

The one idea I want to convey to you in this chapter relates to the thoughts in your mind on a daily basis. As a society we have failed to realize the power of our thoughts, we've failed to realize that the thoughts which dominate our thinking has a direct correlation and connection with the things that we experience in our life. Here are six of the most powerful words that I can relate to you that can change your life and cause a complete metamorphosis in your relationship life.

WE BECOME WHAT WE THINK ABOUT

Where you are right now in your life is a result of the thoughts that have continually dominated your thinking. You cannot wish, hope and desire to find your soul mate and then have thoughts of doubt, uncertainty, fear, unbelief and double mindedness dominating your thought life. Either one thought pattern or the other will dominate your mind and produce results in accordance with the dominating thoughts you're thinking.

"For as he (man) thinketh in his heart, so is he." Proverbs 23:7 You can't think one way and then expect another way to come forth the thoughts you're sowing in your mind you will reap in your life and there's no way around it. You will become what you think. You need to get this scripture in your spirit so it can become a revelation in your heart. You must come into the knowledge that your thoughts are what you, your dating and your relationship life will become. There is no exception to this rule you will become the dominating thoughts that you're thinking.

There is a universal law in the realm of the mind that works the same for all mankind, that law is *"like attract like," "cause and effect," "what you sow, you will reap,"* and *"everything produces after its kind." Genesis1:11-12* An apple tree cannot produce oranges nor can a pecan tree produce plums every tree only produces after its kind. Luke 6:43-44 What you must do is begin to renew your mind, as a Christian you have been given a new spirit and the Spirit of God dwells in your spirit causing your spirit to be alive towards God. Ezekiel 36:26 However, the majority of Christians have failed to renew their minds, God will not renew your mind he has left this task in the hands of each believer and many have done nothing to renew their minds.

The scriptures plainly tells us to *"Be not conformed to this world* (this worlds way of negative thinking) *but be ye transformed* (changed, transfigured, a complete metamorphosis) *by the renewing* (the renovating, the tearing down and away) *of your mind, that ye may prove what is that good, and acceptable and perfect will of God." Romans 12:2-3* Many time people go into prayer lines to get ministers to pray for their situation to change, what needs to change is your thinking ministers need to pray that your thinking change from what it is to what it needs to be.

- *Your thinking needs to change from failure consciousness to success consciousness. Joshua 1:8*

- *Your thinking needs to change from single consciousness to marriage consciousness. Deuteronomy 8:18*

- *Your thinking needs to change from just another date to meeting your soul mate. Romans 8:28*

- *Your thinking needs to change from no prospects to meeting the mate of your soul. Deuteronomy 28:1-14*

- *Your thinking needs to change from I can't to "I can do all things through Christ which strengthens me." Philippians 4:13*

There is nothing true, honest, just, pure, lovely, of good report, of virtue or of praise about or in reference to: just more dates, sin, no prospects, doubt, confusion, or distrust in your Creator. From this day forward change your way of thinking and begin to think relevant to the manual because what you think soon affects your spirit and anything that gets in your spirit whether negative or positive, good or bad is a thousand times stronger than anything in your mind. When something good gets into your spirit then you're able to see the impossible take place and miraculous things begins to happen in your life right before your eyes.

You will be able to say to the Relationship Mountains in your life *"Be thou removed, and be thou cast into the sea; and it shall be done. And all things, whatsoever ye shall ask in prayer, believing shall be done."* Matthew 21:21-22 You will be able to tell the fig tree (your life situations) *"No man eat of thee hereafter for ever. And presently the fig tree will whither away."* Matthew 21:19- 20, Mark 11:12-14

You will be able to *"turn water into wine (turn something natural into something of great value)."* St. John 2:1-11 It all begins with the power to think, most individuals only have mental assent or mental agreement with the word of God, there is no power in this the power is when that word becomes alive in your spirit and from there it affects your entire life.

Your thoughts create your circumstances and lifestyle. Your thoughts create images and the image that you consistently hold in your mind will produce for you according to the image held. Man is not a creature of conditions but instead creates his conditions by his dominating thoughts. In essence, what you think you will soon become *"For as he (man) thinketh in his heart so is he." Proverbs 23:7* As he continues to think so he continues to be. The dominating thoughts of your mind that's hidden from others will attract to you the environment and circumstance which your thoughts secretly longs for whether good or bad. We know what you're thinking by the circumstance and situations that surround your life. If you're dissatisfied with the relationship picture your life is portraying then change it by simply changing your thinking.

Begin to see yourself not as you are but visualize yourself as if you were what you want to be, you can do this by meditation. Here are two scriptures and a method of meditation that can help renew your mind in the area of dating and relationship. *"even God, who quickeneth the dead, and calleth those things which be not as though they were." Romans 4:17*

"This book of the law shall not depart out of thy mouth; but thou shalt meditate therein day and night, that thou mayest observe to do according to all that is written therein: for then thou shalt make thy way prosperous, and then thou shalt have good success." Joshua 1:8 Here is

what to do to position yourself mentally to receive your soul mate into your life: Go into a quite place and begin to meditate on these scriptures, start with the first one in Romans 4:17, repeat this scripture aloud two or three times, then take out the word **calleth** and begin to affirm this word over and over again many times. Afterward imagine yourself in a situation where you're doing things with your soul mate, such as going to the house of God together, going out to dinner together, studying the word together and just doing things where the two of you are enjoying each other. This will have a powerful effect on your mind and your spirit.

Next, do the same with the second scripture in Joshua 1:8, repeat this scripture aloud two or three times, then take out the word success and begin to affirm this word over and over again. Likewise, see yourself in your imagination in a successful relationship; see yourself with the person of your dreams and with the relationship that you have always desired. Imagine it in detail see the surroundings, feel it, smell it, touch it, hear it let it be so real that you can taste its outcome. Do each of these exercise for about five to ten minutes a day two to three times a day and watch the effects of what will begin to happen in your life. The word of God says, *"Meditate upon these things; give thyself wholly unto them; that thy profiting may appear to all."* 1 Timothy 4:15

THOUGHTS CREATES CIRCUMSTANCES

The thoughts that dominate your mind have a direct effect on your circumstances. Man is not a creature of conditions, but instead creates his conditions by his dominating thoughts. The person that continually goes on just another date has created these circumstances by their dominating thoughts. All mankind will eventually have and become that which they secretly think about whether it's just another date or finding their soul mates. The dominating thoughts of their mind that's hidden from others attract to them the environment and circumstances which their thoughts secretly longs for, whether just more dates or your true soul mate.

THOUGHTS CREATES LIFESTYLES

Those dominating thoughts whether positive or negative will soon advance you to the final level of living. This level produces such a stronghold on an individual that it will create a continual lifestyle according to those dominating thoughts. Let your thoughts create the lifestyle that you envision. The lifestyle of not just another date but of finding your ideal soul mate. For your outer circumstances will reflect your inner thoughts.

8
The Power of Imagination

THOUGHTS CREATES IMAGES

As the thoughts are passed down, so is the next level of living that seals the deal unless you break the pattern. The next level of living that's passed down is called imagery. The dominating thoughts over time have formed a picture or image of your relationship life. This image and picture over time in return creates your circumstances. What I want you to understand dear reader is this: The image that you consistently hold in your mind will *produce for you according to the image held.* If you hold a continual image that *God is directing the path of my soul mate and I to each other, a prudent wife is from the Lord, a faithful man is God sent, God has blessed me to find a good thing, and see yourself with your soul mate God will use that image to bring it to pass.* The word **"image"** is the root word of **"imagination"**. The Hebrew definition of the word imagination is *"the squeezing into shape that which is out of shape to mold into a form, to frame."* The imagination that comes from the thoughts you're thinking shapes a picture in your mind of those thoughts and molds those thoughts into a form or frame that's with you consistently. Whether negative or positive it's framed and formed into your mind.

The Greek definition of imagination means, *"to take an inventory, conscience thought."* The proper imagination is vital to finding your ideal soul mate. Your imagination can either steer you toward finding your soul mate or repel you from your soul mate and your soul mate from you. The Greek definition of image is defined as *"a likeness, a profile, representation or resemblance."* The dominating thought of your mind causes an image that creates a likeness, a profile, a representation and resemblance in your outer circumstances.

If you can imagine it you can have it. In the scriptures we have a story of the tower of Babel. Here we have a group of people that had purposed or imagined in their heart to build a tower that would reach up to heaven. However, God had to come down to confound their language in order to stop what they had imagined to do. Their objective was to be unified not for the right reasons but for the wrong reasons. *"And the LORD said, Behold, the people is one, and they have all one language; and this they begin to do: and now nothing will be restrained from them, which they have imagined to do."Genesis 11:6*

However, when you use your imagination you will use it for good. Your imaginations are created by your thoughts and what you have purposed for your relationship life shall happen because you are made in the image and likeness of God. When you imagine thoughts then so shall it be because the greater one is within you. When you use your imagination you are **dating in the spirit** and imagining those things to be as though they were.

9
The Power of Words

"Death and life are in the power of the tongue: and they that loveth it shall eat the fruit thereof." Proverbs 18:21

AFFIRMATION THE KEY TO ATTRACTION

Here is a spiritual principle that is so powerful that it seems to be magical. This principle governs the universe and it can create great change for the individual that uses it, it is called Affirmation or Confession. This principle is a key to bringing about change in your life whether in the form of personal change, bringing new people, things or situations into your life.

Affirmation is speaking forth words out of your mouth about what you want to see manifested in your life. Affirmations are an extremely powerful principle, so powerful in fact that it seems to have the power equivalent to the fairy tale story of Aladdin's Lamp when done properly. When an individual speak forth affirmations they are in effect declaring to God, his creation and the entire universe a statement. Affirmation can also mean to decree a thing. The world of God tells us how God used this principle and made a decree concerning things saying: *"When he made a decree for the rain, and a way for the lighting of the thunder:* **Then did he see it,** *and declare it; he prepared it, yea, and searched it out." Job* 28:26-27 God has also given us this authority to do the same saying; *"Thou shalt also decree a thing, and it shall be established unto thee: and the light shall shine upon thy ways." Job* 22:28. Hallelujah and praise the Lord!

In affirming a thing, it may appear that you're just speaking words into thin air and you're the only one that's hearing the affirmations, decrees or confession, but it's just the opposite. That affirmation, decree and confession that you're speaking forth goes out to God and he responds and causes things to start happening on your behalf. Genesis 1:3-24 The power of confession is only limited by the person's personal conviction and belief that the affirmations are working. The affirmations must not be spoken halfheartedly with doubt, but full of faith that the thing shall come to pass-it shall happen. If you truly believe what you're affirming then you shall receive the confession of your faith. *"And Jesus answering saith unto them, Have faith in God. For verily I say unto you, That whosoever shall say unto this mountain, Be thou removed, and be thou cast into the sea; and shall not doubt in his heart, but shall believe that those thing he saith shall come to pass; he shall have whatsoever he saith." St. Mark* 11:22-23

You will rise or fall according to that which you're confessing. If you start out with a weak confession and don't sense that faith is in it, stop the confession and go into prayer to get into the presence of God. When you feel or sense that you've connected in prayer start your affirmation once again out loud and watch faith come. As those words go forth, God responds and brings the manifestation of that which you desire. Affirmation or confession is the missing revelation in all of life areas. As you begin your confession, let your affirmation be strong and powerful. Be consistent in doing your affirmations. Do them on a daily basis; at night before you go to bed and once again in the morning when you arise and as often during the day as you can. Speak your affirmations clearly and slowly. Affirm them with feeling and meaning. Don't let lifeless and dull words come out of your mouth, but words full of faith and power, strong and mighty. Feel the power behind your words. See them as a declaration and proclamation knowing that you are speaking forth that which you desire to see happen in your life.

Don't miss a day of affirming (*if you miss a day, don't get discouraged and give up, but persevere continually*) because you can never retrieve that day. Daily affirming is vital. It builds up a spirit of consistency that becomes a habit and when something becomes a habit it forms within your character and when your character is formed, it helps creates your destiny. Destiny is not a matter of chance, but a matter of choice. Your destiny is in your hands. God has done his part and has now commissioned you to do yours by letting your words work for you instead of against you.

AFFIRMATIONS ARE FOR YOUR SUCCESS

As you get started with affirmations, *(I will give you an example of an affirmation for attracting your soul mate)* realize that they are a powerful means for conditioning and renewing your mind so that you can begin to think according to that which you desire. Romans 12:1-2 Next to building up your spirit, nothing is more important than a healthy state of mind and as your mind is renewed it in turn affects your spirit and you become strong in both mind and spirit. And then nothing shall be impossible unto you. Mark 11:22-24

GUIDELINES FOR PRACTICING AFFIRMATIONS

Always affirm that something is happening here and now. Do not affirm that something will happen in the future. It's actually a negative confession that says, *"Someday, I will find my soul mate or someday I will be married."* Place the results in today let it be now, *"Now faith is." Hebrew 11:1* One thing we want to bear hard in this section is that it won't happen overnight. It takes time to build the word into your spirit and renew your mind. It won't happen just because you say it one or two times. Understand it happens as you continually affirm it; it will get into your spirit and become a part of you. When your affirmations become a part of you then you shall have that which you've confessed and nothing shall be impossible unto you.

AFFIRMATIONS PLUS ACTION EQUALS SUCCESS

As you perform your affirmations on a daily basis there are several ways that God will bring that which you're affirming to pass. In one instance, you may begin to notice that *"hunches"* or *"inspirations"* may come to you to do certain things that will cause that which you've been affirming to come to pass. Another method God may use is working through other individuals. He may have an individual to tell you something that you need to know that's the answer to what you've been affirming.

He may also use a person to contact you in one manner or another to give you direction about that which you need to know. In most cases the individual being used as an answer may not necessarily know they're the instruments that God is using to bring your affirmation to pass. Only God and your family members will know about your affirmations for you're doing it in secret, but God will reward you openly. Matthew 6:4. God could use a number of methods to bring your affirmation to pass. He is God and he has all the answers and methods needed to make it happen. If God uses the method of hunches or inspirations by speaking to your spirit about something to do or say to bring your affirmation into the external world of reality, don't be *slothful; put it into action immediately. Proverbs 12:24. 27, 15:19, 18:9, 19:15, 24 21:25, 22:13*

The thing to remember is that whichever way God chooses you must take action or all your affirming will have been nothing more than a chasing of the wind. You are affirming something that you desire to see happen in your life now-let it happen. Your affirmation shall come true. It's your job to recognize God's methods and move when he moves, always giving him praise for the answer. When this happens therein lays your destiny and your answer and you shall have that which you desire. The key word here is action. Make that move act now for *"faith without works (action) is dead." James 2:26.* Now be alert for God's method of manifestation.

THE POWER OF WORDS

"Death and life are in the power of the tongue: and they that love it shall eat the fruit thereof." Proverbs 18:21 Your words are full of power and they will bring forth into your life exactly what comes out of your

mouth. Words either create or destroy. They can make your future fruitful or disastrous. You are the architect of your destiny and your words help create your destiny. Your tongue has within it an awesome source of power; James in his epistle spoke to us concerning the power of the tongue. He understood that man has a powerful instrument in his possession. Yet, many times man fails to realize the power of his words. Daily he speaks words of negativity, poverty, death, sickness, dissatisfaction, failure etc... Man continually digs a hole for himself deeper and deeper in every area of his life as he daily affirms and confesses words of death and destruction.

James said, *"For in many things we offend all. **If any man offend not in word,** the same is a perfect man, and able also to bridle the whole body. Behold, we put bits in the horses' mouth, that they may obey us; and we turn about their whole body. Behold also the ships, which though they be so great, and are driven of fierce winds, yet are they turned about with a very small helm, whithersoever the governor listeth. Even so the tongue is a little member, and boasteth great things. Behold, how great a matter a little fire kindleth! And the tongue is a fire, a world of iniquity: so is the tongue among our members, that it defileth the whole body, and setteth on fire the course of nature; and it is set on fire of hell. For every kind of beast, and of birds, and of serpents, and of things in the sea, is tamed, and hath been tamed of mankind: But the* *tongue can no man tame; it is an unruly evil, full of deadly poison. Therewith bless we God, even the Father; and therewith curse we men, which are made after the similitude of God. Out of the same mouth proceedeth blessing and cursing. My brethren, these things ought not so to be." James 3:2-10*

Your words control your life. Up to this point they have controlled your relationship life and have brought to you just more dates instead of helping you find your soul mate. From this day forward, your words shall change and you shall begin to speak forth that which you desire to see manifested in your life. It's time for your joy to be made full, for God is faithful that promised. He said *"So shall my word be that goeth forth out of my mouth: it shall not return unto me void, but it shall accomplish that which I please, and it shall prosper in the thing whereto I sent it." Isaiah 55:11*

ATTRACTING YOUR SOUL MATE
AFFIRMATIONS

"Even God who quickeneth the dead, and calleth those things which be not as though they were." Romans 4:17

AFFIRMATION FOR THE MAN

Father, I thank you for blessing me to meet my soul mate.

God is now directing the path of my soul mate and I to each other. A prudent wife is from the Lord and I thank you Father for my wife. God has blessed me to find my ideal soul mate for He knows where this woman is and he has ordered our steps toward each other and I am so happy. God through His divine intelligence and wisdom is orchestrating our destiny right now. My soul mate and I shall recognize each other immediately.

God has attracted to me my ideal soul mate that is on one accord with me. My soul mate is compatible with me and we blend perfectly together. My soul mate and I love each other and we are the best of friends. Our relationship is based on the word of God and built upon the solid rock, which is Christ. Because I love this woman I can give to her the love, happiness and fulfillment she needs from the human standpoint. This woman appreciates me for me in spite of my failures and shortcoming and, there is a spiritual and soul connection between us. We are irresistibly attracted to each other and enjoy the company of each other. We are kind to one another, tenderhearted, forgiving, even as God for Christ's sake hath forgiven us. We walk in love as Christ has loved us and given himself for us. This woman has qualities and attributes that I desire in my soul mate: she is spiritual, virtuous, harmonious, faithful, prosperous, honest, and loving, a good listener, and a good communicator, peaceful, intelligent, wise, passionate and true. We have confidence in each other and are committed to each other. I thank God for my soul mate and I receive her now.

AFFIRMATION FOR THE WOMAN

Father, I thank you for blessing me to meet my soul mate. God is now directing the path of my soul mate and I to each other. A good godly faithful husband is from the Lord and I thank you Father for my husband. God has brought me to my ideal soul mate for He knows where this man is and he has ordered our steps toward each other and I am so happy. God through His divine intelligence and wisdom is orchestrating our destiny right now. My soul mate and I shall recognize each other immediately.

God has attracted to me my ideal soul mate that is on one accord with me. My soul mate is compatible with me and we blend perfectly together. My soul mate and I love each other and we are the best of friends. Our relationship is based on the word of God and built upon the solid rock, which is Christ. Because I love this man I can give to him the love, happiness and fulfillment he needs from the human standpoint. This man appreciates me for me in spite of my failures and shortcoming and, there is a spiritual and soul connection between us. We are irresistibly attracted to each other and enjoy the company of each other. We are kind to one another, tenderhearted, forgiving, even as God for Christ's sake hath forgiven us. We walk in love as Christ has loved us and given himself for us. This man has qualities and attributes that I desire in my soul mate: he is spiritual, faithful, harmonious, prosperous, honest, loving, a good listener, a good communicator, peaceful, intelligent, wise, passionate and true. We have confidence in each other and are committed to each other. I thank God for my soul mate and I receive him now.

You can also replace anything in this written affirmation that's more to your liking and reword it according to what you desire in your soul mate. You can word it to display qualities and characteristics that you desire in your mate. Make this affirmation one of the first things you do in the morning and the last thing you do before going to sleep, so that it can get into your spirit, which never sleeps and watch God answer you and bring it to pass.

10
Call Them Forth

"Even God who quickeneth the dead, and calleth those things which be not as though they were." Romans 4:17

If you want to see a change in your relationship life then you must realize that this concept of **"Calling Them Forth"** is not a natural act but a spiritual act and it will seem foolish to the natural person and the carnal citizen. The reason it is a spiritual act is because it's of God and God is not natural but He is spirit. When you desire something from God that thing is already yours as a spiritual blessing but it has to be manifested in the natural. The word of God says, *"Blessed be the God and Father of our Lord Jesus Christ, who hath (that's past tense) blessed us with all spiritual blessings in heavenly places in Christ." Ephesians 1:3* The thing that you desire is a spiritual blessing in heavenly places but it's in Christ.

- The husband that you desire is in Christ.
- The wife that you desire is in Christ.

So therefore any person that you date that's outside of Christ is outside of the kingdom and is not a part of the spiritual blessing in heavenly places in

Christ. Citizens of the Kingdom that say they are having a hard time meeting the right person don't understand what they possess.

- They don't understand that it's already done.
- They don't understand that it's easy not hard.
- They don't understand that marriage is a spiritual blessing.
- They don't understand that this thing is done in heavenly places not earthly places.
- They don't understand that it's in Christ the anointed one and his anointing that destroys every yoke of hardship.

As a citizen of the Kingdom the King has given you the authority to be like him. The only way that you will get results like him is to act like him, be like him and do like him. When Jesus was teaching his disciples about faith he said to them, *"Have faith in God." Mark 11:22* The original Greek translation of this verse means to have *"the faith of God."* Only when you have the faith of God can you do the acts of God. Jesus went on the say, *"For verily I say unto you, That whosoever shall say unto this mountain (with the faith of God – and many theologians and others believe that he was talking about a literal mountain), Be thou removed, and be thou cast into the sea; and shall not doubt in his heart, but shall believe that those things which he saith shall come to pass he shall have whatsoever he saith." Mark 11:23*

When it comes to a spouse; marriage falls in the category of things that you can believe for and say. However, this is not a natural belief of just a mental assent with the word of God but an inward spiritual knowing that what you believe shall come to pass without a doubt in your heart. If you can have this kind of supernatural belief then brother/sister go ahead and get your best man or bridesmaid together because you shall be married or bringing your plans to a conclusion within the next 365 days of your inward spiritual knowing.

The manual says, "*(As it is written, I have made thee a father of many nations,) before him whom he believed, even God, who quickeneth the dead, and calleth those things which be not as though they were.*" Romans 4:17 Now here are the translated versions of that scripture in the Phillips, the Message and the Amplified Bible translation.

- *"The whole thing, then, is a matter of faith on man's part and generosity on God's. He gives the security of his own promise to all men who can be called "children of Abraham", i.e. both those who have lived in faith by the Law, and those who have exhibited a faith like that of Abraham. To whichever group we belong, Abraham is in a real sense our father, as the scripture says: 'I have made you a father of many nations'. **This faith is valid because of the existence of God himself,** who can* *make the dead live, and speak his Word to those who are yet unborn." **Phillips***

- *We call Abraham "father" not because he got God's attention by living like a saint, but because God made something out of Abraham when he was a nobody. Isn't that what we've always read in Scripture, God saying to Abraham, "I set you up as father of many peoples"? Abraham was first named "father" and then became a father because he dared to trust God to do what only God could do: raise the dead to life, with a word make something out of nothing. **When everything was hopeless, Abraham believed anyway, deciding to live not on the basis of what he saw he couldn't do but on what God said he would do.** And so he was made father of a multitude of peoples. God himself said to him, "You're going to have a big family, Abraham!" **Message***

- *"As it is written, I have made you the father of many nations. [He was appointed our father] in the sight of God in Whom he believed, **Who gives life to the dead and speaks of the nonexistent things that [He has foretold and promised] as if they [already] existed." Amplified***

As a child of Abraham the father of faith, you are the seed of Abraham. *"Even as Abraham believed God, and it was accounted to him for righteousness. Know ye therefore that they which are of faith, the same are the children of Abraham. So then they which be of faith are blessed with faithful Abraham. And if ye be Christ's then are ye Abraham's seed, and heirs according to the promise."* Galatians 3:6-7, 9, 29 God has given his word on marriage that it is honorable and if you marry you do well. Hebrews 13:4, 1 Corinthians 7:38a So if God has given his word on it then why are citizens of the Kingdom having such difficulty seeing the manifestation of the right spouse coming into their life. One of the reasons is because the citizens of the Kingdom are perishing for a lack of knowledge and they have not been taught how to bring the manifestation forth. Hosea 4:6 Here are some key elements that must be in place for the manifestation to happen.

1. **There must be a word from the Lord.** (We have that word as stated above according to the word God has given about marriage.)

2. **You must believe the word of the Lord.** (But shall believe that those things. Mark 11:23b)

3. **You must say that which you believe not just believe it but it must be a spoken word out of your mouth.** (That whosoever shall say unto this mountain and shall believe that those

things which he saith shall come to pass; he shall have whatsoever he saith. Mark 11:a,c)

Therefore, if you want to see the manifestation of the person that you want to date and conclude with marriage then you must begin to not only believe but call them forth. Even though they are not presently in a manifested form before your eyes at the moment you must begin to:

- *Speak his Word to those who are yet unborn* **(or to those who have yet manifested before your eyes. Calling those things that be not as though they were.) Phillips**

- *When everything was hopeless, Abraham believed anyway, deciding to live not on the basis of what he saw he couldn't do but on what God said he would do. And so he was made father of a multitude of peoples. (Likewise you must not look at what you see – no dates – no potentials – wrong dates – wrong potentials – but you must live on the basis of God's word – marriage is honourable – and if you marry you do well. Then you will see the manifestation of the date – the potential – the right date – the right potential.)*

- *Who gives life to the dead and speaks of the nonexistent things that [He has foretold and promis-*

ed] as if they [already] existed." Amplified (You must believe and know that your dating and relationship life as it exist at the moment even though it's dead or dying you must believe and know that as you call it forth God is speaking of your non-existent date and relationship life that he has promised in his word as if it already existed.

When Abram was getting old in age he and his wife tried to help God with a seed to establish his covenant. Genesis 16:1-3, They tried to do it by natural means just as most citizens try to do natural dating in the hopes of finding a spiritual spouse. The promise that God made to Abram was fulfilled but not by natural means but it was a supernatural act; Abraham was an hundred years old and Sarah was 90. To read more about the promise of God to Abram concerning a son read Genesis 12-18, 21.

- So if you're willing to believe God for a spouse you must do as God and call them forth knowing that it's the father's good pleasure for you to be married. No matter how long you may have been single God can turn this thing around in your favor by supernatural means because: ***of the existence of God himself,*** *who can make the dead live,* *and speak his Word to those who are yet unborn."* **Phillips** *When everything was hopeless, Abraham believed anyway, deciding to live not on the basis of what he saw he couldn't do but on what God said he would do.* **Message** *In the sight of God in Whom he believed, Who gives life to the dead and speaks of the nonexistent things that [He has foretold and promised] as if they [already] existed."* **Amplified**

Call Them Forth

Father God, thank you for your eternal word that shall not pass away. On the basis of what you said you would do and who you are I thank you for my spouse now. I believe that man/woman has come forth in the realm of the spirit and shall be manifested in the natural before my eyes. Today I call into existence that man/woman to come forth that you have ordained for me to marry from the foundations of the world through your omniscience wisdom, omnipotent power and omnipresence spirit. I thank you that he/she is revealed now and I accept and receive him/her and according to your word which never fails to produce results. **For you said, "What things soever ye desire (I desire a husband/wife), when ye pray, believe that ye receive them, and ye shall have them."** **Mark**

11:24 So shall it be and so it is in Jesus Name. Amen.

Continue to call them forth until you see the manifestation of your spouse in physical form before your eyes. For God is faithful that promised.

11
The Power of Meditation

"But his delight is in the law of the LORD; and in his law doth he meditate day and night. And he shall be like a tree planted by the rivers of water, that bringeth forth his fruit in his season; his leaf also shall not wither; and whatsoever he doeth shall prosper." Psalm 1:2-3

Throughout the Bible, we see the term meditation over and over again as the key to success in life. In Joshua 1:8 it says, *"This book of the law shall not depart out of thy mouth; but thou shalt meditate therein day and night, that thou mayest observe to do according to all that is written therein: for then thou shalt make thy way prosperous, and then thou shalt have good success."* Meditation is a lost art in the body of Christ. The devil has made this a most misunderstood topic and has kept the saints away from the use of this powerful spiritual weapon. When you meditate, you imagine and envision in your mind the outcome of a thing as manifest in your spirit. The Hebrew word for meditate means to actually imagine or see a thing as happening; this is nothing more than faith in action. If you want to go from just another date to finding your soul mate, you must first come out in the time of meditation through the use of your imagination. See yourself with your ideal soul mate and get a clear mental picture of it just as it shall be when it happens. Spend time meditating and envisioning you and your soul mate doing the things you would do when you are together in reality. This may be one of the hardest tasks you will ever have to do but if you will be consistent with it you will see the *results "and then thou shalt have good success."* *Joshua 1:8*

See your soul mate and you spending time together, going out to dinner, going to church, going to the movies and enjoying one another. See all this in as precise detail as you possibly can and have a clear mental picture of this as actually happening. Hold consistently to your vision with faith and belief; do not waver in the least *"for he that wavereth is like a wave of the sea driven with the wind and tossed. For let not that man think that he shall receive any thing of the Lord. A double minded man is unstable in all his ways."* *James 1:6-8* Allow this image and vision to get in your spirit. Do not become discouraged if it seems like you're not progressing; the more you meditate and envision the outcome of you and your soul mate, the more it will get in your spirit and become real. Having such times of daily envisioning and meditation evokes the thing that you are meditating upon to come forth in your life. As you envision the outcome as manifested in your imagination, you are calling forth by faith, that which you desire. This is faith in action acting as if your desire is a reality.

- Faith is calling those things that are not as though they were. Romans 4:17

- Faith is moving toward what you hope for just as if you know it shall happen and manifest at the appropriate time.

- Faith is action; it's doing something that draws you toward the manifestation of your beliefs.

- Faith knows that God has already set everything in order and we're walking it out in our everyday lives.

"Now faith is the substance of things hoped for, the evidence of things not seen. For by it the elders obtained a good report. Through faith we understand the worlds were framed by the word of God, so that things which are seen were not made of things which do appear. Let us draw near with a true heart in full assurance of faith, hold fast the profession of our faith without wavering; (for he is faithful that promises)." Hebrews 11:1-3, 10:22-23 What evidence do we have that faith can do what we desire to see happen, the scriptures tell us saying; *"And what shall I more say? for the time would fail me to tell of Gideon, and of Barak, and of Samson, and of Jephthae; of David also, and Samuel, and of the prophets: Who through faith subdued kingdoms, wrought righteousness, obtained promises, stopped the mouths of lions, Quenched the*

violence of fire, escaped the edge of the sword, out of weakness were made strong, waxed valiant in fight, turned to flight the armies of the aliens. Women received their dead raised to life again." Hebrews 11:32-35

If God can do all these things through faith, surely he can orchestrate the destiny of you and your soul mate bringing you both together by his divine understanding and wisdom. Meditation guarantees your success. While Isaac was waiting for Abraham's servant to return with the lady that would be his soul mate and wife, the scriptures say: *"And Isaac went out to meditate in the field at the eventide: and he lifted up his eyes, and saw, and, behold, the camels were coming. And Rebekah lifted up her eyes, and when she saw Isaac, she lighted off the camel. For she had said unto the servant, What man is this that walketh in the field to meet us? And the servant had said, It is my master: therefore she took a vail, and covered herself. And the servant told Isaac all things that he had done. And Isaac brought her into his mother Sarah's tent, and took Rebekah, and she became his wife; and he loved her: and Isaac was comforted after his mother's death." Genesis 24:63-67* Once again, Meditation in action bringing forth success and it always manifests in the external realm of reality.

12
A Soul Mate Chart

A soul mate desire chart is a chart that displays your 10 desires that you want in your soul mate. A soul mate chart is like producing a profile of the person that you desire to find or be found by. Your soul mate chart helps to clarify the type of soul mate you desire so that you will know exactly what you're seeking. Once you get a clear mental image of your soul mate this enables you to present with clarity your desire to God and puts out a blueprint of your desire throughout the earth. Your soul mate desire chart is your detailed outline of your specific soul mate choice. It is your plan of action for finding or being found of your soul mate. It is the essential features or main aspects that you believe will enable you to have a successful and blessed relationship and marriage.

One note that I would like to make is to be always open to God who knows all things from the beginning to the end. Your chart gives God and you something to work with and focus on to create faith in your heart. If one or two out of the ten things does not totally line up but eight or nine things does and you have a witness and peace in your spirit don't try to hold out for all ten. Realize that ultimately God is the only one that knows what you really need and these eight or nine things that he/she possess will be the essential and vital qualities that you will need in your soul mate to enjoy the celebration of love that you need to make it a success. The scripture says, " *A man's heart deviseth his ways: but the LORD directeth his steps.*" Proverbs 16:9

SOUL MATE DESIRE CHART

"Here are my 10 desires that my soul mate possess."

- Spiritual =
- Physical =
- Financial =
- Mental =
- Social =
- Secular =
- Ministry =
- Marital =
- Activities =
- Values =

You can either write them out here or you can take a sheet of paper and write them out. Take out time to meditate on this chart; you can do 20 minutes of daily imagining this person in your life. You can one do a 20-minute session or two 10-minute sessions, whichever is more convenient for you. In your meditation time you will see yourself with this person; you will imagine this person and you enjoying life together in every way. Now, take this time to write out your soul mate chart for your soul mate waits.

13
Twelve Authoritative Prayers to Bind and Blast Away — Just Another Date

"And whatsoever you shall bind on earth shall be bound in heaven." Matthew 16:19

Here are 12 Authoritative prayers that you can use to bind and blast away just more dates. From this day forward begin to take authority over your relationship life and determine your destiny by orchestrating it in prayer. At this point go to God in prayer and confess any known sin to the Lord and repent of anything that may stand between you and God. Ask him to forgive you and cleanse you by his precious blood. Next, take about 5 minutes and begin to spend time in praises to the Lord, thanking him for who he is and what he has done for you and what he shall do for you in orchestrating the destiny of you and your soul mate. Now, enter into this time of prayer with aggressive and bold praying. Go into Spiritual Warfare and pray these prayers repeatedly with determination and faith until you see the manifestation of your desire.

1. **I bind just more dates from coming into my life from this day forward in Jesus name.**

2. I refuse to waste my time with individuals that aren't sent by God to be in my life in the name of Jesus.

3. No weapon that is formed against me shall prosper in the name of Jesus.

4. I reject unrighteous associations that try to become a part of my life in Jesus name.

5. I release myself from the spirit of divorces and unstable relationships in the name of Jesus.

6. Every spirit of instability in relationships I detach myself from you in the name of Jesus.

7. I break the spirit of familiarity that has caused me to attach myself to people that have been wrong for me in the past in the name of Jesus.

8. Every satanic influence that has led me astray in relationships the hand of God is against you in Jesus name.

9. Every satanic deception; the fire of God is against you in Jesus name.

10. Every seducing spirit; the Lord rebukes you in Jesus name.

11. Every hidden agenda come to light and is bound in Jesus name.

12. I reject all that are transformed as an angle of light, but are sent by Satan to destroy and prevent my true marital destiny in Jesus name.

14
Twelve Authoritative Prayers to Loose and Attract Your Soul Mate

"And whatsoever ye shall loose on earth shall be loosed in heaven." Matthew 16:19

Here are 12 Authoritative Prayers you can use to Loose and Attract Your Soul Mate. Go into Spiritual Warfare and pray these prayers in the same manner which you prayed the prayers prior and watch God attract to you your soul mate and life mate.

1. **I loose the Spirit of God to attract to me the individual that God has destined to be my soul mate and life mate in the name of Jesus.**

2. **Father, I commit my life to you and thank you for directing me toward the individual that is my soul mate in Jesus name.**

3. **Father, I give you praise that I'm hidden under your shadow so that only my soul mate can find me in Jesus name.**

4. **The blood of Jesus protects me from every encounter that's not the destiny of my soul**

mate and I in the name of Jesus.

5. My relationship life lives now by the resurrection power of the Lord Jesus Christ.

6. The Holy Spirit of God leads me into all truth in relationships in Jesus name.

7. The angel of the Lord encamps about me and delivers me from every satanic plan in the name of Jesus.

8. Father, I thank you for stretching forth your mighty hand to perform signs and wonders in my relationship life in Jesus name.

9. My prayer now attracts to me the soul mate that God has destined for my life in the name of Jesus.

10. The anointing of God destroys every yoke that comes against me in Jesus name.

11. Father, I thank you for your divine intervention on my behalf in the name of Jesus.

12. Lord, thank you for releasing the spirit of attraction that attracts to me my ideal soul mate in the name of Jesus.

15
The Power of Praise

"He staggered not at the promise of God through unbelief; but was strong in faith, **giving glory to God."** *Romans 4:20*

Praise is a missing spiritual weapon in the lives of the citizens of the Kingdom. As a citizen you must use this awesome weapon to get victory in your dating and relationship situation. There is power in praise, not in the praise that comes forth after a victory has been won but the praise that comes forth before the victory or while the battle is going on. I can't think of a better display of praise before victory than the story of Jehoshaphat when he was confronted by the armies that were coming after him. Within this story you will see how God wrought victory through praise, not by natural weapons but by the spiritual weapon of praise. Your victory in dating and relationship will come also through praise!

So the story goes; *It came to pass after this also, that the children of Moab, and the children of Ammon, and with them other beside the Ammonites, came against Jehoshaphat to battle. Then there came some that told Jehoshaphat, saying, There cometh a great multitude against thee from beyond the sea on this side Syria; and, behold, they be in Hazazontamar, which is Engedi. And Jehoshaphat feared, and set himself to seek the LORD, and* *proclaimed a fast throughout all Judah. And Judah gathered themselves together, to ask help of the L*ORD*: even out of all the cities of Judah they came to seek the L*ORD*. And Jehoshaphat stood in the congregation of Judah and Jerusalem, in the house of the L*ORD*, before the new court, And said, O L*ORD *God of our fathers, art not thou God in heaven? and rulest not thou over all the kingdoms of the heathen? and in thine hand is there not power and might, so that none is able to withstand thee?*

Art not thou our God, who didst drive out the inhabitants of this land before thy people Israel, and gavest it to the seed of Abraham thy friend for ever? And they dwelt therein, and have built thee a sanctuary therein for thy name, saying, If, when evil cometh upon us, as the sword, judgment, or pestilence, or famine, we stand before this house, and in thy presence, (for thy name is in this house,) and cry unto thee in our affliction, then thou wilt hear and help. And now, behold, the children of Ammon and Moab and mount Seir, whom thou wouldest not let Israel invade, when they came out of the land of Egypt, but they turned from them, and destroyed them not;

*Behold, I say, how they reward us, to come to cast us out of thy possession, which thou hast given us to inherit. O our God, wilt thou not judge them? for we have no might against this great company that cometh against us; neither know we what to do: but our eyes are upon thee. And all Judah stood before the L*ORD*, with their little ones, their wives, and their children. Then upon Jahaziel the son of Zechariah, the son of Benaiah, the son of Jeiel, the son of*

Mattaniah, a Levite of the sons of Asaph, came the Spirit of the LORD in the midst of the congregation;

And he said, Hearken ye, all Judah, and ye inhabitants of Jerusalem, and thou king Jehoshaphat, Thus saith the LORD unto you, Be not afraid nor dismayed by reason of this great multitude; for the battle is not yours, but God's. To morrow go ye down against them: behold, they come up by the cliff of Ziz; and ye shall find them at the end of the brook, before the wilderness of Jeruel. Ye shall not need to fight in this battle: set yourselves, stand ye still, and see the salvation of the LORD with you, O Judah and Jerusalem: fear not, nor be dismayed; to morrow go out against them: for the LORD will be with you. **(When you begin to do spiritual dating God steps in on your behalf because you're a citizen of the Kingdom and you're acknowledging him and using the weapons of the word to gain victory. You are not using natural means to try and manifest a spiritual thing; therefore as you acknowledge him he will direct your paths. God even told them where to find them — at the end of the brook, before the wilderness of Jeruel — he also knows where your Soul Mate and Life Mate is at this very moment.)**

And Jehoshaphat bowed his head with his face to the ground: and all Judah and the inhabitants of Jerusalem fell before the LORD, worshipping the LORD. And the Levites, of the children of the Kohathites, and of the children of the Korhites, **stood up to praise the LORD God of Israel with a loud voice on high.** *And they rose early in the* *morning, and went forth into the wilderness of Tekoa: and as they went forth, Jehoshaphat stood and said, Hear me, O Judah, and ye inhabitants of Jerusalem;* **Believe in the LORD your God, so shall ye be established; believe his prophets, so shall ye prosper.** *And when he had consulted with the people, he appointed singers unto the LORD, and that should* **praise** *the beauty of holiness, as they went out before the army, and to say,* **Praise the LORD;** *for his mercy endureth for ever.*

And when they began to sing and **to praise,** **(your dating and relationship victory is in your right now praise—don't wait until the battle is over shout now)** *the LORD set ambushments against the children of Ammon, Moab, and mount Seir, which were come against Judah; and they were smitten. For the children of Ammon and Moab stood up against the inhabitants of mount Seir, utterly to slay and destroy them: and when they had made an end of the inhabitants of Seir, every one helped to destroy another. And when Judah came toward the watch tower in the wilderness, they looked unto the multitude, and, behold, they were dead bodies fallen to the earth, and none escaped. And when Jehoshaphat and his people came to take away the spoil of them, they found among them in abundance both riches with the dead bodies, and precious jewels, which they stripped off for themselves, more than they could carry away: and they were three days in gathering of the spoil, it was so much.(Victory is waiting your praise) And on the fourth day they assembled themselves in the valley of Berachah; for there they blessed* *the* LORD: *therefore the name of the same place was called, The valley of Berachah, unto this day.*

Then they returned, every man of Judah and Jerusalem, and Jehoshaphat in the forefront of them, to go again to Jerusalem with joy; for the LORD *had made them to rejoice over their enemies. And they came to Jerusalem with psalteries and harps and trumpets unto the house of the* LORD. *And the fear of God was on all the kingdoms of those countries, when they had heard that the* LORD *fought against the enemies of Israel. So the realm of Jehoshaphat was quiet: for his God gave him rest round about.* 2 Chronicles 20:1-30

Likewise God is ready to give you rest in your dating and relationship life. However, your rest will only come as you spiritual date and allow God to lead and guide you. Jehoshaphat would have never got victory with natural weapons against this army he needed supernatural help from God. In your dating and relationship situation some of you desire to be married but have been single for 5, 10, 20 + years and you still see no happening on the horizon. Your breakthrough will come as you apply spiritual dating to your situation. We know a lady that desire to be married but has been single for 30 + years and she still say that she is waiting on the Lord. Not realizing that the Lord is waiting on her.

Your victory is in your praise, if you want to see the manifestation of God then begin now to give God praise for your husband/wife. Remember, when God saw the singing and praises of Jehoshaphat and Judah "*the LORD set ambushments against the children of Ammon, Moab, and mount Seir, which were come against Judah; and they were smitten. For the children of Ammon and Moab stood up against the inhabitants of mount Seir, utterly to slay and destroy them: and when they had made an end of the inhabitants of Seir, every one helped to destroy another. And when Judah came toward the watch tower in the wilderness, they looked unto the multitude, and, behold, they were dead bodies fallen to the earth, and none escaped. And when Jehoshaphat and his people came to take away the spoil of them, they found among them in abundance both riches with the dead bodies, and precious jewels, which they stripped off for themselves, more than they could carry away: and they were three days in gathering of the spoil, it was so much."*2 Chronicles 20:22-25 Get your praise on now and give the King the glory due his name for you shall not need to date as the world do *for the battle is not yours, but God's (the King). 2 Chronicle 20:15c*

16
The Song of Solomon

"The voice of my beloved! Behold, he cometh leaping upon the mountains, skipping upon the hills. My beloved is like a roe or a young hart: behold, he standeth behind our wall, he looketh forth at the windows, shewing himself through the lattice. My beloved spake, and said unto me, Rise up, my love, my fair one, and come away."
Song of Solomon 2:8-10

The closest idea we have of a harmonious and compatible relationship of two people in love is exemplified in the scriptures according to the Song of Solomon. Here we have King Solomon and the Shulamite woman that have found the mate of their soul in each other. Here we have two people that are obviously soul mates. The communication and attraction between these two people displays love of the highest order; it shows respect, consideration, passion, compassion, kindness, unselfishness, patience, temperance, faith, hope and belief.

Notice the terminology which they use and the easy display of verbal affection to one another, the honesty, sincerity and excitement of just being in one another's presence. We don't attempt to interpret the words of these two individuals that are wonderfully in love. We just give it to you as it is and allow the Holy Spirit to enlighten your mind and speak to your spirit as you read it. Notice the love and beauty of it all as we listen to two people that are immensely in love with one another as it should be. Listen as the emotions run high and the feelings of each are spoken effortlessly. There is no holding back here because each desires the other to know what they think and how they feel. Read it slowly and observe the words they're speaking.

Let us now behold "The song of songs, which is Solomon's. Let him kiss me with the kisses of his mouth: for thy love is better than wine. Because of the savour of thy good ointments thy name is as ointment poured forth, therefore do the virgins love thee. Draw me, we will run after thee: the king hath brought me into his chambers: we will be glad and rejoice in thee, we will remember thy love more than wine: the upright love thee. I am black, but comely, O ye daughters of Jerusalem, as the tents of Kedar, as the curtains of Solomon. Look not upon me, because I am black, because the sun hath looked upon me: my mother's children were angry with me; they made me the keeper of the vineyards; but mine own vineyard have I not kept.

Tell me, O thou whom my soul loveth, where thou feedest, where thou makest thy flock to rest at noon: for why should I be as one that turneth aside by the flocks of thy companions? If thou know not, O thou fairest among women, go thy way forth by the footsteps of the flock, and feed thy kids beside the shepherds' tents. I have compared thee, O my love, to a company of horses in Pharaoh's chariots. Thy cheeks are comely with rows of jewels, thy neck with chains of gold. We will make thee borders of gold with studs of silver. While the king sitteth at his table, my spikenard sendeth forth the smell thereof. A bundle of myrrh is my well-beloved unto me; he shall lie all night betwixt my breasts. My beloved is unto me as a cluster of camphire in the vineyards of En-gedi. Behold, thou art fair, my love; behold, thou art fair; thou hast doves' eyes. Behold, thou art fair, my beloved, yea, pleasant: also our bed is green. The beams of our house are cedar, and our rafters of fir. I am the rose of Sharon, and the lily of the valleys. As the lily among thorns, so is my love among the daughters. As the apple tree among the trees of the wood, so is my beloved among the sons.

I sat down under his shadow with great delight, and his fruit was sweet to my taste. He brought me to the banqueting house, and his banner over me was love. Stay me with flagons, comfort me with apples: for I am sick of love. His left hand is under my head, and his right hand doth embrace me. I charge you, O ye daughters of Jerusalem, by the roes, and by the hinds of the field, that ye stir not up, nor awake my love, till he please.

The voice of my beloved! behold, he cometh leaping upon the mountains, skipping upon the hills. My beloved is like a roe or a young hart: behold, he standeth behind our wall, he looketh forth at the windows, shewing himself through the lattice. My beloved spake, and said unto me, Rise up, my love, my fair one, and come away. For, lo, the winter is past, the rain is over and gone; The flowers appear on the earth; the time of the singing of birds is come, and the voice of the turtle is heard in our land; The fig tree putteth forth her green figs, and the vines with the tender grape give a good smell. Arise, my love, my fair one, and come away. O my dove, that art in the clefts of the rock, in the secret places of the stairs, let me see thy countenance, let me hear thy voice; for sweet is thy voice, and thy countenance is comely.

Take us the foxes, the little foxes, that spoil the vines: for our vines have tender grapes. My beloved is mine, and I am his: he feedeth among the lilies. Until the day break, and the shadows flee away, turn, my beloved, and be thou like a roe or a young hart upon the mountains of Bether. By night on my bed I sought him whom my soul loveth: I sought him, but I found him not. I will rise now, and go about the city in the streets, and in the broad ways I will seek him whom my soul loveth: I sought him, but I found him not. The watchmen that go about the city found me: to whom I said, Saw ye him whom my soul loveth? It was but a little that I passed from them, but I found him whom my soul loveth: I held him, and would not let him go, until I had brought him into my mother's house, and into the chamber of her that conceived me. I charge you, O ye daughters of Jerusalem, by the roes, and by the hinds of the field, that ye stir not up, nor awake my love, till he please.

Who is this that cometh out of the wilderness like pillars of smoke, perfumed with myrrh and frankincense, with all powders of the merchant? Behold his bed, which is Solomon's; threescore valiant men are about it, of the valiant of Israel. They all hold swords, being expert in war:

every man hath his sword upon his thigh because of fear in the night. King Solomon made himself a chariot of the wood of Lebanon. He made pillars thereof of silver, the bottom thereof of gold, the covering of it of purple, the midst thereof being paved with love, for the daughters of Jerusalem. Go forth, O ye daughters of Zion, and behold King Solomon with the crown wherewith his mother crowned him in the day of his espousals, and in the day of the gladness of his heart. Behold, thou art fair, my love; behold, thou art fair; thou hast doves' eyes within thy locks: thy hair is as a flock of goats, that appear from mount Gilead. Thy teeth are like a flock of sheep that are even shorn, which came up from the washing; whereof every one bear twins, and none is barren among them. Thy lips are like a thread of scarlet, and thy speech is comely: thy temples are like a piece of a pomegranate within thy locks. Thy neck is like the tower of David builded for an armoury, whereon there hang a thousand bucklers, all shields of mighty men. Thy two breasts are like two young roes that are twins, which feed among the lilies. Until the day break, and the shadows flee away, I will get me to the mountain of myrrh, and to the hill of frankincense.

Thou art all fair, my love; there is no spot in thee. Come with me from Lebanon, my spouse, with me from Lebanon: look from the top of Amana, from the top of Shenir and Hermon, from the lions' dens, from the mountains of the leopards. Thou hast ravished my heart, my sister, my spouse; thou hast ravished my heart with one of thine eyes, with one chain of thy neck. How fair is thy love, my sister, my spouse! How much better is thy love than wine! and the smell of thine ointments than all spices! Thy lips, O my spouse, drop as the honeycomb: honey and milk are under thy tongue; and the smell of thy garments is like the smell of Lebanon. A garden inclosed is my sister, my spouse; a spring shut up, a fountain sealed.

Thy plants are an orchard of pomegranates, with pleasant fruits; camphire, with spikenard, Spikenard and saffron; calamus and cinnamon, with all trees of frankincense; myrrh and aloes, with all the chief spices: A fountain of gardens, a well of living waters, and streams from Lebanon. Awake, O north wind; and come, thou south; blow upon my garden, that the spices thereof may flow out. Let my beloved come into his garden and eat his pleasant fruits. I am come into my garden, my sister, my spouse: I have gathered my myrrh with my spice; I have eaten my honeycomb with my honey; I have drunk my wine with my milk: eat, O friends; drink, yea, drink abundantly, O beloved. I sleep, but my heart waketh: it is the voice of my beloved that knocketh, saying, Open to me, my sister, my love, my dove, my undefiled: for my head is filled with dew, and my locks with the drops of the night. I have put off my coat; how shall I put it on? I have washed my feet; how shall I defile them?

My beloved put in his hand by the hole of the door, and my bowels were moved for him. I rose up to open to my beloved; and my hand dropped with myrrh, and my fingers with sweet smelling myrrh, upon the handles of the lock. I opened to my beloved; but my beloved had withdrawn himself, and was gone: my soul failed when he spake: I sought him, but I could not find him; I called him, but he *gave me no answer. The watchmen that went about the city found me, they smote me, they wounded me; the keepers of the walls took away my veil from me. I charge you, O daughter of Jerusalem, if ye find my beloved, that ye tell him, that I am sick of love.*

What is thy beloved more than another beloved, O thou fairest among women? what is thy beloved more than another beloved, that thou dost so charge us? My beloved is white and ruddy, the chiefest among ten thousand. His head is as the most fine gold, his locks are bushy, and black as a raven. His eyes are as the eyes of doves by the rivers of water, washed with milk, and fitly set. His cheeks are as a bed of spices, as sweet flowers: his lips like lilies, dropping sweet smelling myrrh. His hands are as gold rings set with the beryl: his belly is as bright ivory overlaid with sapphires. His legs are as pillars of marble, set upon sockets of fine gold: his countenance is as Lebanon, excellent as the cedars. His mouth is most sweet: yea, he is altogether lovely.

This is my beloved, and this is my friend, O daughters of Jerusalem. Whither is thy beloved gone, O thou fairest among women? whither is thy beloved turned aside? that we may seek him with thee. My beloved is gone down into his garden, to the bed of spices, to feed in the gardens, and to gather lilies. I am my beloved's, and my beloved is mine: he feedeth among the lilies. Thou art beautiful, O my love, as Tirzah, comely as Jerusalem, terrible as an army with banners.

Turn away thine eyes from me, for they have overcome me: thy hair is as a flock of goats that appear from Gilead.

Thy teeth are as a flock of sheep which go up from the washing, whereof every one beareth twins, and there is not one barren among them. As a piece of a pomegranate are thy temples within thy locks. There are threescore queens, and fourscore concubines, and virgins without number.

My dove, my undefiled is but one; she is the only one of her mother, she is the choice one of her that bare her. The daughters saw her, and blessed her; yea, the queens and the concubines, and they praised her. Who is she that looketh forth as the morning, fair as the moon, clear as the sun, and terrible as an army with banners? I went down into the garden of nuts to see the fruits of the valley, and to see whether the vine flourished, and the pomegranates budded. Or ever I was aware, my soul made me like the chariots of Ammi-nadib. Return, return, O Shulamite; return, return, that we may look upon thee. What will ye see in the Shulamite? As it were the company of two armies. How beautiful are thy feet with shoes, O prince's daughter! the joints of thy thighs are like jewels, the work of the hands of a cunning workman. Thy navel is like a round goblet, which wanteth not liquor: thy belly is like an heap of wheat set about with lilies.

Thy two breasts are like two young roes that are twins. Thy neck is as a tower of ivory: thine eyes like the fishpools in Heshbon, by the gate of Bath-rabbim: thy nose is as the tower of Lebanon which looketh toward Damascus. Thine head upon thee is like Carmel, and the hair of thine head like purple; the king is held in the galleries. How fair and how pleasant art thou, O love, for delights! This thy stature is like to a palm tree, and thy breasts to clusters of grapes. I said, I will go up to the palm tree, I will take hold of the boughs thereof: now also thy breasts shall be as the clusters of the vine, and the smell of thy nose like apples; And the roof of thy mouth like the best wine for my beloved, that goeth down sweetly, causing the lips of those that are asleep to speak.

I am my beloved's, and his desire is toward me. Come, my beloved, let us go forth into the field; let us lodge in the villages. Let us get up early to the vineyards; let us see if the vine flourish, whether the tender grape appear, and the pomegranates bud forth: there will I give thee my love. The mandrakes give a smell, and at our gates are all manner of pleasant fruits, new and old, which I have laid up for thee, O my beloved. O that thou wert as my brother, that sucked the breasts of my mother! when I should find thee without, I would kiss thee; yea, I should not be despised. I would lead thee, and bring thee into my mother's house, who would instruct me: I would cause thee to drink of spiced wine of the juice of my pomegranate.

His left hand should be under my head, and his right hand should embrace me. I charge you, O daughters of Jerusalem, that ye stir not up, nor awake my love, until he pleased. Who is this that cometh up from the wilderness, leaning upon her beloved? I raised thee up under the apple tree: there thy mother brought thee forth: there she brought thee forth that bare thee. Set me as a seal upon thine heart, as a seal upon thine arm: for love is strong as death; jealousy is cruel as the grave: the coals thereof are coals of fire, which hath a most vehement flame.

Many waters cannot quench love, neither can the floods drown it: if a man would give all the substance of his house for love, it would be utterly contemned. We have a little sister, and she hath no breasts: what shall we do for our sister in the day when she shall be spoken for? If she be a wall, we will build upon her a palace of silver: and if she be a door, we will inclose her with boards of cedar. I am a wall, and my breasts like towers; then was I in his eyes as one that found favour. Solomon had a vineyard at Baalhamon; he let out the vineyard unto keepers; everyone for the fruit thereof was to bring a thousand pieces of silver. My vineyard, which is mine, is before me: thou, O Solomon, must have a thousand, and those that keep the fruit thereof two hundred. Thou that dwellest in the gardens, the companions hearken to thy voice: cause me to hear it. Make hast, my beloved, and be thou like to a roe or to a young hart upon the mountain of spices." Song of Solomon 1-8

17
Hello Soul Mate

"And the LORD visited Sarah as he had said, and the LORD did unto Sarah as he had spoken. For Sarah conceived, and bare Abraham a son in his old age, at the set time of which God had spoken to him." Genesis 21:1-2

What good is a word if it does not come to pass? You can be assured that it's not a word that the King has spoken because the word that the King speaks he is able to make it good. The manual says, *"The King, God is not a man, that he should lie; neither the son of man, that he should repent: hath he said, and shall he not do it? or hath he spoken, and shall he not make it good?"* Numbers 23:19 The whole purpose of this book is for you to meet your Soul Mate and Life Mate. However, we chose to obey the King in showing you how it's done according to the manual. Let's go over the things we have learned in this book. We have learned about:

1. The King and the Kingdom

2. The Natural Realm

3. The Spirit of Fear

4. The Spiritual Realm

Now we come to the conclusion and final chapter, **"Hello Soul Mate."** If you have applied the things that you learned in this book you should be in a mindset of expectation and vision. You should be expecting to say hello to your Soul Mate and Life Mate at any moment. Expectation means to look forward to something, to anticipate something. To have vision means to have revelation and insight and without this you will perish in your dating and relationship life. As a result of what you have learned in this book you should have vision like never before. No longer will you grope around like a non-believer or carnal citizen without vision, their dating and relationship life is perishing.

1. Without vision they can't see what God is trying to show them.
2. Without vision they can't hear what God is trying to telling you.
3. Without vision they're stumbling all over the place.
4. Without vision they have no restraint.
5. Without vision things are running wild in their life.
6. Without vision they have nothing to pursue.
7. Without vision their life is out of control.
8. Without vision they're walking in darkness.

This is your time to receive what God has for you; your soul mate is waiting. This is your time and the soul mate that you desire is also desiring you, the soul mate that you're seeking is also seeking you, the soul mate that you're longing for is also longing for you. Go forth now and say hello to your soul mate and life mate. If you're at home go to your door as an act of faith and open the door and greet your soul mate by saying, "Hello Soul Mate." It's an act of faith but God take the foolish things to confound the wise, it's Spiritual Dating.

MORE KINGDOM BOOKS AVAILABLE AND OTHERS COMING SOON

1. **Kingdom Dating 2**—*Dating for Citizens of the kingdom of God.*

2. **Kingdom Dating 3**-- *Dating a citizen of the kingdom for the purpose of marriage.*

3. **Kingdom Marriage: The Wife's Manual**-- *The newlywed wife guide for citizens of the kingdom for a successful and blessed first and second year.*

4. **Kingdom Marriage: The Husband's Manual** – *The newlywed husband's guide for citizens of the kingdom for a successful and blessed first and second year.*

5. **Kingdom Marriage—Not to Your Soul Mate** – *Married but not to your Soul Mate—you can still make it work.*

6. **Kingdom   Marriages   Getting   Wealthy** – *Financial & Material Prosperity*

7. **Kingdom Marriages In Ministry** – *Co-Laborers Together In the Work of The Lord.*

8. **Kingdom Marriages Enjoying Each Other** – *Vacation Spots, Restaurants, Outings, Hotels etc...*

9. **Kingdom Marriages Living Healthy** – *God Wants You to Have Long Life and Good Health.*

10. **Kingdom Marriages Bible Study & Prayer Manuel** – *Your Spiritual Weapons to Live Victoriously.*

Peace and Blessings Throughout Your Life!

Website and Email Information

www.soulmatesolutions.org

kingdomdating@yahoo.com

Phone: 919-283-9118

www.ingramcontent.com/pod-product-compliance
Lightning Source LLC
LaVergne TN
LVHW021458080426
835509LV00018B/2328